The Christian
And The Law

The Christian And The Law

Selected Red Mass Sermons

of

John Wright
Bishop of Pittsburgh

Fides Publishers, Inc.
Notre Dame, Indiana

BY THE SAME AUTHOR:
WORDS IN PAIN

All royalty proceeds accruing to the author from the sale of this book will be paid to the Catholic Institute of Pittsburgh, Inc., for works of religion, charity, and education.

Library of Congress Catalog Card Number: 62-20572
Designed by Harvey Satenstein
MANUFACTURED IN THE UNITED STATES OF AMERICA BY
BOOK CRAFTSMEN ASSOCIATES, INC., NEW YORK

Christo Regi

. . . Tibi voléntes súbdimur,
Qui iure cunctis ímperas:
Haec civium beátitas
Tuis subésse legibus . . .

Preface

It has long been evident that the Most Reverend John Wright, once auxiliary Bishop of Boston, later first Bishop of Worcester, and now Bishop of Pittsburgh, appreciates the importance of the function of the law in our local, national, and international society. He was a member of the commission of leading citizens, lawyers, and law professors which made a survey of the judicial system in Massachusetts in 1954. He has delivered many notable addresses to lawyers, judges, and public officials on formal occasions.

Several of his addresses relating to the law during the past twelve years have been delivered as sermons at the annual Red Mass which is celebrated in many cities from coast to coast. This volume consists of nine of these sermons. I was privileged to be present when some of these, and when still others not here published, were delivered.

[VII]

It is most gratifying to observe that the vigor, strength, and eloquence of the spoken word have not been diminished in the change to the printed word.

Bishop Wright, as these sermons amply disclose, is a great advocate. As is not uncommon with great advocates, the qualities of the man shine through his advocacy; patriotism, scholarship, and priestly zeal pervade the book. Recognizing as he does the significance of the role of the law in society, Bishop Wright states with fervor and conviction the case for religion as a spiritual force in the life of the individual lawyer, in the life of the profession itself, and in the life of the nation upon which the law and lawyers have their impact.

He does more. He reminds us of the religious heritage which belongs to us as a nation. He recalls to us the publicly professed faith which our forefathers had in Almighty God; he would never have us forget the efficacy of prayer in the discovery of our fair land, in the founding and formation of the Republic, in the establishment and molding of its institutions, and in the development of our national character.

He does still more. He seeks to awaken all Americans, and to alert the legal profession in particular, to the stark danger to our country from the advancing "aggressive secularism." That the danger is real and that the secularism is new and boldly aggressive there now can be no doubt. In the summer of 1962 the country was startled when our highest court took a long, perhaps fateful, step toward a judicially imposed secularism which would do violence to the traditions of our people, Christian and Jewish alike, in whose lives not only private but public and collective prayer has always been welcomed, practised and cherished as part of America's national life. The militant proponents of the new secularism have avowed their intention to press relentlessly until the constitutional prohibition against the establishment of a state religion is transmuted into a declaration that in all public institutions in this nation, down to the smallest hamlet, the existence of God must be ignored.

The publication of this compact volume is therefore most opportune. While each sermon carries its own distinctive and timely message, the book, in total effect, is a trumpet call. The call is not in quavering or uncertain accents, nor does it come too late. Rather, in clear and unfaltering tones, it sounds a new reveille, a reawakening to the priceless treasure of our national spiritual heritage and a warning against whatsoever would debase or destroy it. May the call reverberate and evoke a response throughout our blessed land.

PAUL G. KIRK
Justice, Supreme Judicial Court
Commonwealth of Massachusetts

Credits

The Red Mass Sermons collected in *The Christian and the Law* were delivered by Bishop Wright at the following times and places:

CHAPTER ONE, *"The Supremacy of Law,"* in St. Mary's Cathedral, San Francisco, October 5, 1954.

CHAPTER TWO, *"The New Secularism in America,"* at the 1959 convention of the American Bar Association in Miami, Florida.

CHAPTER THREE, *"Prayer in the American Tradition,"* in St. Paul's Cathedral, Pittsburgh, on September 17, 1959.

CHAPTER FOUR, *"The Roots of Democracy,"* in St. Paul's Cathedral, Pittsburgh, on November 1, 1960.

CHAPTER FIVE, *"The Common Good,"* in St. Ignatius Church, Boston, on September 30, 1950.

CHAPTER SIX, *"The Reign of Law,"* in St. Paul's Cathedral, Pittsburgh, on October 3, 1961.

CHAPTER SEVEN, *"The Philosophy of Responsibility,"* in the crypt of the National Shrine of the Immaculate Conception, Washington, D. C., in 1954.

CHAPTER EIGHT, *"Fear and Love in the Observance of Law,"* in the Cathedral of the Immaculate Conception, Denver, on November 5, 1961.

CHAPTER NINE, *"St. Thomas More and the Modern Lawyer,"* in St. Paul's Cathedral, Worcester, Mass., on May 10, 1956.

Contents

I. The Supremacy of Law 1

II. The New Secularism in America 11

III. Prayer in the American Tradition 22

IV. The Roots of Democracy 32

V. The Common Good 41

VI. The Reign of Law 56

VII. The Philosophy of Responsibility 64

VIII. Fear and Love in the Observance of Law.... 76

IX. St. Thomas More and the Modern Lawyer... 85

The Supremacy of Law

CHAPTER I

EACH YEAR THIS VOTIVE ACT OF ADORATION brings to the altar of the living God the representatives of the judiciary, uniting them in spiritual fellowship with those who, across the ages, have called down the blessings of the Almighty on the evolution of our law in the universities and halls of justice of Bologna, Paris, and Oxford, in the Inns of Court of England and the law faculties of continental Europe.

We in America do well so to associate ourselves with those holy men out of the past who still bow with you before their God and yours, and answer, I have no doubt, their devout *Amen* to the prayer for you intoned at this altar a few moments ago: *"Deus qui corda fidelium* — O God, Who didst instruct the hearts of the faithful by the light of the Holy Spirit, grant us by that same Holy Spirit always to relish what is right and just and ever to rejoice in His consolation! Who livest and reignest world without end!"

You need, as did they who centuries ago first planned this Votive Mass, the guidance of the Holy Spirit of God. But, it is no less true that in a real and basic sense God needs you. God works through secondary causes. It is by men, not angels, that the kingdom of God is brought to pass on earth.

Wherever the truth is made manifest and by whatever man; wherever the good is vindicated and in whatever worthy cause; wherever the beautiful is brought to perfection, whoever be the worker, there God Himself is at work. "Now there are varieties of gifts, but the same Spirit; and there are varieties of ministries, but the same Lord; and there are varieties of workings but the same God, who works all things in all . . . and all of these things are the work of one and the same Spirit" (Rom. 12: 6, 11).

The gifts which your vocation requires of you and the works you do as makers and judges of the law are so close to those of God Himself as to give them some shadow, however faint, of the divine Majesty itself. You are the wielders, in varying degrees, of sovereignty; you interpret and apply, you bind under and loose from, that positive civil law which is the codification in our society, as God has given us to achieve it, of the natural law which the Creator has implanted in the innermost hearts of men.

The temporal authority you wield derives so intimately

from God that Bossuet could call those who hold such authority and administer its law "men like unto God."

You attain your offices and commissions by democratic election or by duly prescribed appointment; you are answerable to those who designate or elect you. But your sovereignty is still from God; there is no true authority which is not divine, no trust which is not sacred, no stewardship which is not answerable ultimately to God.

In a democracy, those who hold divine authority, for however brief a time, are responsible to God for the liberties of the people whom they rule.

Liberty, no less than authority, is a divine perfection. Indeed, perfect liberty is proper to God alone, for only in God does there exist, in absolute degree, that self-dominion which is implied in the very concept of liberty. The mastery which in God makes perfect His liberty is identified with the divine sovereignty — and so in God freedom and sovereignty, liberty and authority are flawlessly integrated, wonderfully harmonized.

Among men, however, mastery, whether of self or of society, is never complete and never without challenge, and so freedom among men is never perfect. Among men authority, too, is always shaded with imperfection; it is sometimes suspect and often defied.

Liberty and authority, so perfectly reconciled in God, are, even among men, correlative attributes. But historically there frequently exists in all forms of society a disturbing tension between the claims of authority and the pursuits of liberty.

Our fathers in this new world of America knew that the divine attributes of liberty and authority, analogously present among men, could only be reconciled in our topsy-turvy world if God Himself would somehow work among us to accomplish their reconciliation. Our fathers did not believe that it is enough for God to be in His Heaven in order that all be well with the world.

They knew that Heaven and earth must work together if the earth is ever to achieve something, at least, of the order which prevails in Heaven and if the sons of men are finally to win the freedom of the sons of God.

They knew that, as order is Heaven's first law, so law is the condition, the essential condition, of order on earth.

Our forefathers, for reasons of prudent realism, provided in their constitutions for the separation of the organized Church and the organized State; but their idealism, even in temporal matters, was nonetheless informed and inspired by the Judeo-Christian tradition, and especially by the Revelation transmitted by the Church; and so there is reflected in the wise laws which they wrote for the preservation of both liberty and authority a blend of the divine and the human, a happy medley of the hopes of earth and the will of Heaven.

The men who wrote our basic laws realized that in God's holy providence all society, religious and civil alike, and all legal traditions, both of authority and of liberty, exist for the perfection of human personality. They would have understood the magnificent implications of the doctrine which Pope Pius XI so wonderfully summarized: "It is according to the dictates of reason that ultimately all things should be ordained to man as a person, that through his mediation they may find their way back to the Creator. In this wise we can apply to man, to the human person, the words of the Apostle: 'All things are yours, whether it be Paul or Apollo, or Cephas, or the world, or life, or death, or things present, or things to come; for all are yours; and you are Christ's; and Christ is God's'" (Encyclical *Divini Redemptoris*).

Hence the necessity, clear from reason and confirmed by revelation, that the law weigh all things in the scale that measures their effects on human personality.

The celebrated French Declaration of the Rights of Man, despite its debatable premises and its lamentable omissions, enunciated at least one proposition that, so far as it goes, is beyond dispute: "Ignorance of and contempt for the rights of man are the chief cause of public evils and the corruption of governments."

The authors of our basic law understood that a truly humane civilization dedicated to respect for the rights of man must have a government of laws, not of men — of objective, constitutional statutes, not subjective, arbitrary impulses, however high-minded, however immediately beneficial. They resolved that the moods and passions of the people must never be permitted to overthrow the institutions which represent their own deliberate development and their own deepest convictions.

Our written laws, basic among them our Constitution as interpreted by the judiciary, constitute at once the fruit of our deepest convictions and the safeguard of their survival. And these objective, constitutional controls our forefathers committed to the bench and bar — to you. By your oaths you are bound to preserve them.

It was an act of almost superhuman prudence which placed in the hands of judges the security of our liberties. Elsewhere, even in constitutional governments, the judicial power is invariably subordinate to the legislative. Even in England, as Chief Justice Taney once remarked, the courts are bound to enforce the acts of Parliament, even should they believe them to conflict with Magna Charta or the Petition of Rights. But our forefathers built more wisely; they acknowledged in the executive and legislative branches of government only those powers specifically delegated to them in the Constitution.

Many of these wise men had long since ceased, for reasons of sad history, to catch the overtones of divine authority in the pronouncements of the Roman Pontiff; but all of them, I think, would have endorsed with full understanding the declaration broadcast some time ago from the Vatican, a declaration directed primarily, of course, against the dictatorships of the moment, but setting forth a principle contradicting all arbitrary and totalitarian government. Said the Vatican radio: "The Pope indicts attempts to subordinate juridical and legislative activities to the requirements of particular groups, classes, or movements, as these must be subordinated only to the establishment of justice and to the service of society as a whole. . . . The Pope condemns those who dare to place the fortunes of whole nations in the hands of one man alone, a man who as such is the prey of passions, errors, and dreams. . . . It is essential that a pre-established set of laws be placed above the governor and the governed alike, far outside the reach of arbitrary action."

Mindful of just such salutary truths, our forefathers providentially empowered their courts to test, in accordance with well-settled and familiar principles of law and equity, every demand for further power, for political action, for departure from tradition made by any executive, however wise or however popular, or by any legislature, however capable or however representative.

Through their courts, as our forefathers constituted them, the American people themselves protect themselves against themselves. Our courts represent, as one critic has said, the settled habits of thought and action of our people.

An executive might be influenced powerfully by the disillusion or the dreams of the moment; he might be deluded by the siren song of the elusive future and forget the warning voice of the sane past. A Congress might be stampeded by a madcap outcry, and even a majority might be found to demand crude and unwise legislation.

And so our forefathers looked to the judiciary to decide whether a popular but passing whim might be leading to political action which would contradict the constitutional guarantees of personal liberty and political security. If so, even the majority would have to withdraw its demand or give its apparent wish time for the patient meditation and cautious procedure required in order to revise the Constitution.

But to override the Constitution, to despise the tradition, this would be revolution, and our forefathers, though they might readily revolt against men, were at all times wary about revolution against the law. For them no political dream could be so dazzling, no social need so urgent, no executive so capable, no majority so overwhelming, that they would permit any or all of these to put aside the codified tradition of the Constitution and its authentic interpretation. That is what our forefathers meant when they planned a government of laws, not of men.

This conservatism of our forefathers was not designed to enslave us in the name of the past, but was calculated to save us from enslavement in the name of the future. It recognized that hard-won liberties can be speedily lost under the seduction of easily promised future freedoms; that the God-given heritage of the past and the sacred liberties of the present can easily be sacrificed in the name of a future which may never be, which perhaps were better not.

The conservatism of our forefathers is particularly saving in time of social crisis; it reminds us that there will be, when the tumult and the shouting dies, no new heaven and no new earth. It reminds us that the citizens of any brave new world to be will still be men, not gods.

It reminds us that any future world can only be built out of whatever good survives from the old. It warns us never to hold lightly the good which our forefathers built so patiently here in this continent; never to gamble with the liberties which are the heart and soul of that good; never to permit the religious faith which taught us those liberties to grow cold; never to forget the blessings on this land by which Almighty God has confirmed the wisdom of those who, building it, honored Him and His chief creature, the human person.

It may be that you do not always discern the blessing of God on the faith of our fathers. But if you doubt the wrath of God on those who thus propose to forget that faith and to desert its legal corollaries, then I invite you to advert once more to the military, economic, and political preoccupations which you left behind you at the doors of this church and to which you must soon return.

No defense of Christianity and of the values which it taught our forefathers could be more effective than the present straits to which new prophets, contemptuous of the faith, have reduced the world. Should contemplation of the disasters which infidelity to the laws of nature and of nature's God has released upon whole areas of society dishearten you in your effort to cleave to the ancient traditions of our people, know that as God was with our fathers, so will He be with us. Take heart from the memory of how our forefathers made possible the fulfillment, on these shores, of the prophetic word of the

Psalmist: "Blessed are the people whose God is their Lord." Learn from the history of this land and never forget it, that for those who love God all things work together unto good. For those who love God seek His will in free but faithful submission to the supremacy of law, natural and revealed, human and divine: the law which you duly apply and by which you devoutly live.

The New Secularism in America

CHAPTER II

THE SOLEMN GATHERING FOR THE RED Mass, offered for the members of the bench and the bar, permits me to serve as spokesman for those who bear witness to the law of God in speaking to those who are privileged to write, interpret or apply the law of the land.

There was a time in our country when any dichotomy between the law of God and the law of the land was rarely real and never intentional. It was assuredly never as systematic as recent developments under the influence of increasingly aggressive secularism have sometimes made it seem.

Quite the contrary, those who bore witness in America to the law of God were the more inspired to preach and to pray for enthusiastic, wholehearted obedience to the law of the land precisely because in so doing they were logically defending the civil corollaries of their sacred teachings. At the same time, those whose public duties bound them to the enactment, interpretation, and enforcement of public law consciously sought to promote piety and virtue, not merely to define the limits of the law's negative interest in these; they did so convinced that thus they best served the civic common good and the rights and needs of human personality adequately considered.

We cannot too often recall that although our forefathers, for reasons of prudent realism, provided in their constitutions for the separation of the organized Church and the organized State, their idealism, even in temporal matters, was the product of the Judeo-Christian revelations as transmitted by the Church. This is why there is reflected in the basic laws which they wrote a blend of divine faith and human wisdom, a medley of earth's best hopes and Heaven's revealed will.

The United States Supreme Court, speaking by Mr. Justice Brewer, on one occasion declared in remarkably direct terms the religious, indeed, the organized Christian character of the American tradition within which the law of the land became an effort by positive human legislation to apply the broad precepts of the law of conscience and the law of God, unto the service of virtue and the perfection of personality.

The Court said:

> If we pass beyond these matters to a view of American life as expressed by its laws, its business, its customs, and its society, we find everywhere a clear recognition of the same truth.

Among other matters note the following: The
form of oath universally prevailing, concluding
with an appeal to the Almighty; the custom of
opening sessions of all deliberative bodies with
prayer; the prefatory words of all wills, "in the
name of God, Amen"; the laws respecting the
observance of the Sabbath, with a general cessa-
tion of secular business, and the closing of
courts, legislatures, and other similar public as-
semblies on that day; the churches and church
organizations which abound in every city, town
and hamlet; the multitude of charitable organizations existing everywhere under Christian
auspices . . . . these and many other matters
which might be noticed add a volume of un-
official declarations to the mass of formal utter-
ances that this is a Christian Nation.

So far the words of the Court; nor is their import
obscure. Without prejudice to the strict religious tolerance
that obtains for all faiths, without disparagement of the
notable influence on our national life of the devout members of other faiths, this nation was considered in its
inspiration and its life a Christian nation.

The traditional habits of mind and attitudes of our
people, as well as their institutions and laws, were those
which have been developed under the dominance of the
Christian faith, embryonic in the promises made to Israel,
born together with the Church on Pentecost two thousand
years ago, and coming to maturity with a strength so
vital that it communicated itself to the cultures of those

peoples who once made Europe great and America possible.

The men who most contributed to the early building of our nation feared God. They did so with a holy and a wholesome fear, and because they did, they wrote into the preamble of the constitution of my own native state, typical of that of many, devout words of homage to their Creator together with a recognition of their dependence on Him and an explicit prayer for His direction in the mighty task of building their Commonwealth.

They feared God, and so they did not talk glibly of a mere freedom to worship God, a freedom which they had scant intention of exercising or implementing. Rather, they wrote in the second article of the Massachusetts constitution words of right, but also of duty. They said: "It is the right as well as the duty of all men in society publicly and at stated seasons to worship the Supreme Being, the great Creator and Preserver of the universe . . ." Such men feared God! They would have found unintelligible the suggestion that there is and need be no connection between the law of God and the law of the land, between personal morality and civic virtue of the citizen.

Every American who walks in their tradition and who shares either their patriotism or piety acknowledges that morality and legality, like Church and State, have separate areas of competence, separate formalities and separate sanctions; but the legislators, justices, and lawyers who fashioned our basic legal traditions would have been appalled by the contention, now so often, so glibly, and so effectively advanced, that such separation means divorce of the law of the land from the law of God, and "that religious morality and civic virtue spring from totally distinct and completely separate, if not mutually antagonistic, sources," as a contemporary secularist asserts.

Nothing could be further from the mind of the men who wrote the basic laws of our states, the Founding Fathers who placed the Bible, God's law, on the very rostrum where they took their oath to defend the law of the land. They would have had no trouble defining as blasphemous or vicious any efforts to represent them as being indifferent to the relation of civil obligation to moral duty, the law of the land to the rule of reason and the rule of reason to the law of God.

They would have resented as intellectually fraudulent the current kind of censorship by exclusion, "thought-control" by silent, careful editing, reflected in a recent book which purports to offer collegians and others the basic thought of Thomas Jefferson and yet edits out all the characteristic references to God, to virtue, to morality, and to the blessings of religion which the author of the Declaration of Independence made so frequently.

Fortunately the bench and bar are not yet without men who dare—and the word "dare" is not too strong—to speak in the spirit and accent of the founders and fashioners of our legal heritage, as did that Protestant judge on the West Coast who recently braved the wrath of the new secularists, and incurred it, by suggesting from the bench that a Catholic boy would improve his regard for the law of the land by increasing his respect for the law of God and his consequent attendance at Sunday Mass.

The Catholic bishops of America have drawn the fire of the insurgent secularists, and of some of their own people, because of their defense of the traditional American concept of the sovereignty of God over Church and States alike, the concept of the necessary relation between all ultimately valid laws and the postulates of the law of God.

Sometimes criticism of the Catholic bishops for their opposition to the spirit of secularism has come from surprising, even disappointing, quarters. But equally often, there is consoling evidence that in the appeal for the spiritual philosophy of the Founding Fathers, Protestants and Catholics can and do speak as one. Nor are they alone.

For example, when the Catholic hierarchy issued its collective pastoral on the damage of secularism in the national life, Dr. Eugene Carson Blake, an executive of the Presbyterian Church in the United States, made it clear that his co-religionists, whatever their positions on other and secondary matters, would stand together with us in what he called the "common fight against the inroads of humanistic secularism and the attacks of atheistic communism" which would "undermine the spiritual foundations upon which our freedoms, civilization and our culture necessarily rest."

Those foundations have always included the recognition that there are not two standards of morality. There is only one. It is God's standard. That standard is the norm of rectitude, righteousness, and justice. That single standard covers all man's relations to God, to himself, and to the world about him.

It applies to every conceivable situation in life—in the home, in business, in the school, in the political field, or in the field of entertainment. The thoughts of men are many; the will of God is one—and so by its very nature, God's standard precludes that duplicity which not only tempts man to live his life on two levels, one of morality, the other of legality, but beguiles him into thinking that this can be done without any compromise of moral principles.

Such a two-faced way of living explains the scandalous anomaly evident at times in our national life of paying lip service to God while failing to honor His claims in daily life. Of such a way of life, the god is neither Jehovah nor Jesus Christ; it is Janus—and we do well to pray earnestly and resolve mightily that we will always be at one in repudiating the two-faced god of the pagans.

That God's standard has disappeared more and more from our national life is due, as the Catholic bishops and the Presbyterian moderator both bear witness, to that totalitarian secularism and practical atheism which rule out all idea of the sovereignty of God. Against such lamentable pretensions we must bear, in season and out, uncompromising witness to God's dominion over all the work of His hands, ourselves and our societies included. We must be vigilant and prompt to affirm the sovereignty of God and His place in human affairs wherever opportunity presents. Where there is talk of the service we owe anything less than God, we must recall the principle by which St. Joan of Arc resolved every question pertaining to rival loves and loyalties: *The Lord God must be first served.*

The undermining of the standard of God's law in temporal affairs has been further hastened by the denial or neglect of the primacy of the spiritual, with a consequent debasing of human personality and degrading of human society. Ours is in large part a technical civilization, a "know-how" rather than a "know-why" civilization; it is, therefore a civilization in which material and mechanical values inevitably tend to dominate thought and action. Excessive emphasis on "know-how," to the exclusion of speculation on "know-why," has tended to produce the cult of the body, the predominance of the material, the worship of the gadget, an indifference to the spiritual and a repudiation of the moral.

We may note this in professional discussions, especially those pertaining to sociology, medicine, and politics. Take, for example, the problem of social disease, which touches on all three. It offers an obvious example of how solutions on the material level alone, scientific techniques of "know-how" without reference to moral considerations of "know-why," are woefully inadequate as means to the protection or the perfection of human personality. Obviously in the case of the treatment of social disease, the problem is never purely scientific — and neither can the solution be. The actions and offenses involved are never merely legal questions; they always include moral elements that are at the heart of the matter.

And yet, in *Social Medicine,* a publication of the New York Academy of Medicine, I read this significant paragraph typical of the neo-secularist approach:

> Not long ago health administrators thought that if only some excellent curative agent were available to treat venereal disease cases, the problem could be solved fairly promptly. Now penicillin is providing more satisfactory treatment than the most sanguine might have dared hope, and yet we find that instead of diminishing, the venereal disease rate is rising. Recently the venereal disease director of one of our best state health departments said that he is convinced that the problem is much broader than that of treatment alone.
>
> There must be a concerted assault on all aspects of the situation if effective control is to be secured. Treatment must be pushed as completely and carefully as possible. There must also be an attack by all community agencies which can help to remove conditions leading to promiscuity. Sex education must be improved and decent recreational opportunities made available. Home ties will have to be strength-

ened, prostitution repressed and intensive efforts
made to rehabilitate socially those now engaged
in prostitution and perversion.

Now what we all, you and I, will find discouraging,
what, as a matter of candid fact, we must find down-
right dishonest in this paragraph, as in the whole report,
is the studious avoidance of the use of the word "moral."
There is talk of "family relations," "prostitution," numerous other notions all involving morality, moral codes,
moral judgment, moral relations, moral questions — but
a careful and hardly accidental omission of the word
"moral." The omission is significant; I am afraid it is
symptomatic. It is also fatal; fatal not merely to morality,
but in final terms, to the work, prestige, and interest of
medicine, sociology, and law.

It exemplifies that repudiation of the primacy of the
spiritual which is the unhappy by-product of a "know-
how" without "know-why" civilization, and of the effort
to divorce the laws and procedures of the land from the
law and the Providence of God. It reflects the pretensions and the aggressive advance of the new secularism
in America.

It should be our common concern to give the lie to
any such pretense of the independence of valid legal
philosophy from moral philosophy, and divorce of valid
human law from the ultimate law of God. For all human
laws, whether ecclesiastical or civil, have their source in
God's law; otherwise they become inevitably meaning-

less. All human sanctions ultimately depend for their force and meaning on the sanction of the conscience that is sensitive to the law of God.

The appeal to that conscience must be made by both the teachers of the law of God and the practitioners of the law of the land, or all law is in peril. So intimately bound up with one another are the laws of the land and the law of God, that he who mocks the one, undermines the other, while he who serves either becomes the noble servant of both.

Prayer in the American Tradition

CHAPTER III

"MAY THE LORD OUR GOD BE WITH US, AS He was with our fathers, and not leave us, nor cast us off:

"But may He incline our hearts to himself, that we may walk in all his ways, and keep his commandments, and his ceremonies, and all his judgments which he commanded our fathers. . . .

"That all the people of the earth may know, that the Lord He is God, and there is no other besides him" (3 Kings 8:57-60).

These words are taken from the prayer that Solomon offered in the name of his nation in the days when Israel, having escaped from subjection to Egypt, was building its temples, its cities, and its proud traditions in restored faith and new freedom. This prayer of Solomon, as the prayers of all who held public power in ancient Israel, reveals the place of prayer in the formation and the life of a free, strong people.

When the Puritan founders of Boston were choosing a motto to sum up the spiritual idealism behind their civic hopes and to suggest the roots in piety which they knew any strong political commonwealth must have, they chose a line from this same prayer of Solomon. The Protestant citizens inscribed on the seal of the American city the Latin phrases in which the Catholic tradition had preserved the Hebrew Scriptures: *"sicut cum patribus nostris, sic sit Deus nobiscum:* May the Lord our God be with us, as he was with our Fathers!" It is a motto like to those of many American cities and states. It proclaims the place of prayer in the American tradition.

That place had been foreshadowed from the very beginning. Time was when the rich continent which has become the fair hope and firm strength of America was inhabited by scattered tribes of Indians. The ways of these people were primitive and savage, but the Indians are remembered in the American tradition as having been, at their noblest and best, a prayerful people. All the cruelty of the Indian is forgotten when we gaze on Cyrus Dallin's superb sculpture of the Indian brave astride his horse, his arms outstretched in prayerful "Appeal to the Great Spirit." The statue represents the place of prayer even in the primeval tradition of America.

That place is unmistakably affirmed on the first pages of recorded American history. The opening of this continent to permanent colonization began with the coming of Columbus. The very name of his flagship was an implicit prayer, but Professor Morison gives us the explicit words of the daily prayer that was the inspiration, often the consolation of his historic journey: "May Jesus with Mary be with us on our way!"

The Holy Sacrifice of the Mass, offered immediately upon the landing of Columbus, marked at once the climax of the Old World story and the beginning of the New World saga. The names which Catholic discoverers and missionaries gave to so many of our rivers and lakes, as well as to the first settlements they established here, still speak to us of the place of prayer in the American tradition; they are the names of the saints, the Mother of Christ, and the mysteries of the Faith from which their prayers drew strength.

When Protestant Christians came to New England and later to this part of America, it was the same. The place of prayer in the American tradition is proclaimed in the Mayflower Compact at Plymouth Rock, in 1620, the opening words of which —" In the name of God, Amen!" — have become as a devout refrain in American wills and public documents for generations since. For the inscription on the Liberty Bell at Independence Hall in Philadelphia, our Founding Fathers chose a line of Sacred Scripture and thus made an ancient Hebrew prayer the proclamation of our highest political hopes.

The place of prayer in our tradition and the part of prayer in the forging of our national strength were early acknowledged by our first president in his First Inaugural

Address. Speaking in New York in 1789, George Washington said: "No people can be bound to acknowledge and adore the Invisible Hand which conducts the affairs of men more than those of the United States. Every step by which they have advanced to the character of an independent nation seems to have been distinguished by some token of providential agency."

And so, in that same First Inaugural Address, Washington began and ended with a prayer. It is good to recall his words, both because of their dignity and grace and because they are reminders of the place of prayer in the authentic American tradition. Washington said:

> . . . it would be peculiarly improper to omit in this first official act my fervent supplications to that Almighty Being Who rules over the universe, Who presides in the councils of nations, and Whose providential aids can supply every human defect, that His benediction may consecrate to the liberties and happiness of the people of the United States a Government instituted by themselves for these essential purposes, and may enable every instrument employed in its administration to execute with success the functions allotted to his charge. In tendering this homage to the Great Author of every public and private good, I assure myself that it expresses your sentiments not less than my own, nor those of my fellow-citizens at large less than either.

Our First President ended his Inaugural with these words:

> . . . I shall take my present leave; but not with-
> out resorting once more to the benign Parent
> of the Human Race in humble supplication
> that, since He had been pleased to favor the
> American people with opportunities for delib-
> erating in perfect tranquility, and dispositions
> for deciding with unparalleled unanimity on a
> form of government for the security of their
> union and the advancement of their happiness,
> so His divine blessing may be equally conspic-
> uous in the enlarged views, the temperate con-
> sultations, and the wise measure on which the
> success of this Government must depend.

In all the greatest moments of our national history, from that day to this, the place of prayer in the American tradition has been manifest. Someone has taken the trouble to gather in a single book prayers taken from the pronouncements of all our presidents. It has been noted that each has declared his belief that God exists, that we have duties and obligations toward God, and that this nation owes to God its debt of prayerful grati-tude for the blessings He has showered upon it. The prayers of our presidents are personal efforts to persevere in the example of George Washington, but they are also reflections of the religious conviction and prayerful spirit of the American people from whom our presidents come, of whom they are the elected representatives and to whom they are responsible for their public conduct and for the spirit in which they exemplify our nation to the world.

The most grave crises in the history of our nation have invariably found its people turning to prayer, each time to rise from their prayers confirmed in their faith and renewed in their freedom. In each of these crises, our leaders have personified the prayerful spirit of the nation and the place of prayer in our tradition. In the hour of the revolution which gave birth to the nation, Washington prayed at Valley Forge. In the deliberations out of which came the charters of our nation's existence and rights, Franklin called for prayer. No president spoke of prayer more fervently or had public recourse to prayer more frequently than did the Great Emancipator under whom our national union was preserved, so that this nation, under God, had a new birth of freedom. Under a Presbyterian president, who quoted in his declaration of war some ringing words of Martin Luther, America entered the first of the modern World Wars which threatened that freedom; other presidents echoed in their prayers for America the words of the Hebrew prophets or the Catholic saints.

How could it be otherwise? For our government, as President James Madison noted, while pledging to avoid "the slightest interference with the rights of conscience or the functions of religion, so wisely exempted from civil jurisdiction," has nonetheless always "encouraged [this nation] to feel [confidence] in the guardianship and guidance of that Almighty Being Whose power regulates the destiny of nations, Whose blessings have been so conspicuously dispensed to this rising Republic, and to Whom we are bound to address our devout gratitude for the past, as well as our fervent supplications and best hopes for the future."

Recent days have found among us one who affects, at least, to despise the power of prayer. Where the American tradition would impel us to speak of God as the Father of Nations and of prayer as the language in which, though many peoples, we speak as one family to our Heavenly Father, the Communist First Secretary, on his visit to America this year, spoke significantly and calculatingly of "Mother Earth" as our common parent and the sole source of our strength; this earth which, in an eventual lifelessness and bleakness like to those of the moon, will be the inevitable grave of our happiest and most sublime hopes if Khrushchev be right and George Washington wrong. Washington, calling upon us to link our hopes for peace and progress to prayer, called God the "benign Parent of the Human Race," and would have esteemed both the earth and the moon to be the coldest and most cruel of prisons if God were absent and the public prayer of religion mocked.

Americans will not accept a despotism like that of which the Communist is at once the spokesman and the agent. All our traditions of freedom revolt against the very thought of falling victims to Communism's political pretensions. But Americans, mindful of the place of prayer in our national tradition, will resist with no less passion and determination the negative, enslaving cynicism that speaks to us only of the earth as our parent and is silent about God, the Father under whom we have our true fraternity. All our traditions of faith impel us to resist Communism's false and perilous concept of God, of nature, and of man.

In the tradition of our people and of their representative leaders since first America began to be, in the tradition that was prefigured on our shores before America began to be, we must pray during these crucial days for America and for the society of which America is a part. We shall pray that God will be with us as He was with our fathers, inclining our hearts to Himself, that we may walk in all His ways and keep His commandments; that we may somehow manifest Him and His power to those who come among us, so "that all the people of the earth may know that the Lord is God and there is no other besides him."

When our recent Communist visitor passed under the main arch leading into the Union Station in Washington, he could have seen three inscriptions declaring the dependence of our republic on the guiding hand of Almighty God. They were carved there, when the station was built, as acknowledgments of that dependence and as expressions of the place of piety and prayer in our tradition. One is from the Old Testament and announces the supreme dominion of God; it rebukes all totalitarianism that mocks the claims of conscience and the primacy of

the spirit. The second is from the lips of Jesus Christ
and proclaims the relation of His saving truth to every
form of freedom. The third sums up the motivation of
our people: "Let all the ends thou aimest at be thy
country's, thy God's, and truth's."

Everywhere in the national capital, as in most places
throughout the land, our visitor could find like reminders
of this interrelation of faith and freedom, of freedom
and faith, which is the heart not only of the American
tradition but of every valid hope of mankind everywhere.
But if monuments were all that were needed to keep
alive awareness of God and the spirit of prayer, then the
visitor from behind the Iron Curtain would have had
them a-plenty in his own cities and in every land over
which his airplane passed. Even their skylines still reveal
reminders of the cross of Christ and their ancient monuments are still marked by neglected religious symbols,
Jewish and Christian, still cherished in secret by millions
of his subjects and still shared between them and us.

But monuments, like quotations out of the past, are
not enough. There is needed the living, constant witness
of intense personal faith, unashamedly proclaimed in
public prayer such as that of our forefathers, if America's
piety is to be effective at home or persuasive abroad. It
is to stimulate such faith, to nourish such piety and to
sound the call to such prayer in our own community,
that we have gathered for this Votive Mass of the Holy
Spirit. In it, as in all the prayers offered in public and
in private throughout our community, let us beg God

to strengthen and guide those who hold in their hands our civil liberties and our spiritual traditions. Let us pray that they may keep strong in their minds and hearts the religious virtues on which our liberties and our common good depend for survival in a world easily tempted to forget faith and to neglect freedom. In times so perilous to all we hold dear, as believers in God and as free men, may the Lord God be with us, as He was with our fathers!

The Roots of Democracy

CHAPTER IV

OURS IS THE OLDEST DEMOCRACY IN EXISTence. For more than 180 years America's democratic form of government has withstood the tests and trials which have greatly altered or completely overthrown every other form of government in the world. The present need of our democracy is not for eloquent praise, but for honest appraisal of its original roots and of the present so real dangers to its survival.

We know the meaning of democracy; its philosophical meaning corresponds exactly with its dictionary definition and its literal derivation from the Greek. It means a people's government. It is the organized expression of the people's inherent right to rule. Its flowering has been political and social, but its roots are religious, even theological. The origin of its basic concept goes back to God, not to any convention of men, and to the Garden of

Eden, not merely to Philadelphia, Runnymede, or Athens.

God made man in His own image and likeness. In the hour of human creation, God gave man stewardship over all else that He had made, commanding mankind to "increase and multiply and fill the earth and subdue it and rule over it" (Gen. 1:28). In that primeval command God, who possesses all authority, delegated to man a true sovereignty over creation. In that delegation to mankind are the conceptual roots of democracy.

It is well to dwell on this point for a moment. God made man like to Himself and constituted him lord of all creation. *The earth is the Lord's and the fullness thereof,* but He has given it to man, all men, as an inheritance. The fish, flesh, and fowl, the fruits and treasures of the earth belong to man and all men have right of access to them. All men are equally creatures of the Lord and heirs to the dominion over the earth delegated by God to mankind's primeval ancestors. All have their share in the dominion which God gave man in the hour of creation. Democracy, providing for the exercise of such dominion, is therefore consistent with the original order of things described in the first verses of Sacred Scripture.

Accordingly, the divine right of men to rule themselves and to share in the ruling of all creation dates not from 1775, 1620, 1215 or any other arbitrary date; it dates from that primeval hour when God gave the goods of the earth and dominion over them not to a king nor a class, but to man himself and as such.

With that dominion and the rights implicit in it, there came another right; it, too, was implanted by God in our very nature. Man was created intelligent and therefore both empowered and required to use reason. The right to rule the earth is a right that all men share; this fact requires that the manner of its exercise be worked out in common counsel and in an organized, rational fashion. The complex business of harmonizing each one's right with all men's rights — the need of orderly procedures in correlating the rights of all with the rights of each — required that men provide for a due order in the practical performance of the common responsibility toward the common good. And so, from the beginning, men were impelled by nature to choose rulers, judges, magistrates, and other agents of mankind to do for all in orderly fashion what no one would have the right to do except by the mandate of all. To each of those thus chosen to act for the general community, man gave as much or as little delegated authority as need dictated. This was the seed of democratic government, its forms and patterns. Like democratic authority itself, this, too, goes back beyond recorded history to the hour and, indeed, the nature of creation.

These are fundamental concepts, familiar to every devout man who philosophizes about society. If we recall them now, it is because such things may be so well known that they are no longer thought about; they are taken for granted, and thus they are forgotten. It is because these principles were frequently forgotten in the past that they were so often violated and lost.

The first thing men tended to forget was their right to choose their rulers. They let other men look out for that, and so they gradually lost its exercise themselves. They saw their kings assume the right to rule as if it were their due, their very own. Thus was born autocracy, the origins and growth of which Cardinal O'Connell set forth with logic and brevity in an Independence Day address on the subject to which today we direct our attention.

Autocracy, the Cardinal noted, probably did not start by usurpation. Its first step was doubtless popular neglect of government. The people cared first for their own personal affairs. Nor has usurpation usually been even the second step on the way to tyranny. The supreme exaltation of kings came from those among the people who found that this fitted best their selfish interests. A centralized, efficient rule frequently procures such great advantages that it sweeps men into unrestricted power almost despite themselves. Fatally, autocracy takes over then.

As masters of the people, instead of their delegated legislators, rulers begin now to replace the laws of nature and of nature's God with their own whim or fancy. Once, for example, they even seized the power of God and styled themselves Divine. Such were the Roman Julius and the Roman Augustus who both styled them-selves *Divus Caesar,* The Divine Caesar. Here is a typical instance of self-assumed Divine Right. We name them from among numerous examples because they, most of all, have left their mark upon the civil government of the world.

But the Caesars were not the last, as they had not been the first, to arrogate to themselves the title of divinity. Even in Christian times people became so forgetful of their own sovereignty and rights that they accepted talk of "the divine right of Kings" in Catholic France and in Protestant England. Sometimes when secularists concoct a "religion of democracy," as in America there is a present trend to do, political democracy comes perilously close to the same totalitarian pretense.

But in the reign of the first Augustus there was born One who put in a single formula the only truly effective check on autocracy. These are the words of Christ who came to bring back justice as well as love to all humanity: "Render to Caesar the things that are Caesar's, and to God the things that are God's." These words were the real Bill of Rights for democracy. They vindicated the rights of God in human society. They restricted human rule to things of earth and therefore gave protection to the sound premises of democracy.

The story of our American democracy illustrates the familiar truths that I have been recalling. For the two hundred years between the Wars of the Roses and the English Revolution, the power of the crown in England increased at the expense of the people's rights. The absolutism which the Tudors practiced was made a theory of government under the Stuarts. The Church was made subordinate to the king's rule and even the king's whim; Parliament ceased to be the voice of the people, the royally established Church and the debilitated Parliament became tools of, rather than controls on the tyrant. There was no freedom of spirituals, no freedom of temporals; the crown controlled worship, silenced free speech, censored the public press, confiscated private property and even violated the basic right to life.

This was the autocracy from which many free spirits fled to develop in the New World their own idea of freedom. It was the system which Englishmen in the homeland overthrew by regicide. It was the system, based on a theory of divine right of kings, which finally drove the Stuarts from the throne. The English Revolution gave England a new constitution — a compromise with kings, a bill of rights for men. Deep, bitter, and lasting hostility to the Tudors and their successors was the inheritance of the American colonists. Passionate attachment to their liberties, as granted them by the English Constitution, marked the beginning and the growth of the specifically American polity. Then, when under George III, autocracy flourished anew in destruction of the colonists' rights, there came the American Revolution.

This time there was no compromise. The fathers of this Republic had no intention of merely securing a bill of rights, compelling grants from an unwilling king. They overthrew the autocracy of a tyrannical monarchy and made a valiant, historic declaration of the rights of man. They established here a union of free and independent states, imperfect in its initial vision of the full range of freedom, no doubt, but capable of leading to ever more real freedom in speech, in press, in use of property, in enjoyment of home and in development of person. The security of those freedoms they placed in the wisdom of sound laws rather than the reliability of even righteous men. They gave us a government of laws, not men, and these laws they spun around certain convictions which amounted to dogmas with them.

These "dogmas" embraced the three fundamental principles of our democracy — all men created equal, government dependent on the consent of the people, and the right of free assembly. On these three principles the American Constitution was worked out, a constitution which became the practical result of theoretical principles of government that religious revelation and right reason had illumined from the beginning.

It is possible that we, too, may forget the ultimate sources of our rights. If we are born with equality it is because we are equally the creatures of God. Now, it is possible to forget God and God's law, and so the first and greatest danger to our democracy is irreligion or religious indifference. People speedily forfeit their own dignity who forget the God who is the source of that dignity.

The consciousness of the presence of God and awareness of our relationship to God do not fade of a sudden; they yield slowly but surely to the rival spirit of preoc-

cupation with self. Such a spirit has no place for the law
of God because it is a spirit that will not be retarded in its
selfish course. Thus it is that simple greed and vanity
unchecked finally bring to pass the denial of God Himself, first in practice, then in doctrine.

Wherefore, irreligion, infidelity, and atheism constitute
perils to democracy greater than any others. They undermine the very source of rights. Unless the thought of
God as the Supreme Ruler is clear in the mind and
obedience to His law is firm in the heart, we speedily
find might replacing right and human equality an empty
phrase. Unless God and His law hold their place of
primacy among us, we come to think of ourselves alone
and set the stage for the moral and political heresies
which destroy democracy from the Left or the Right,
but totally in either case.

The second thing that we must not forget is our right
to judge justly our civic rulers. They are the appointees
and the agents of the people. They are responsible to
the people. We choose them to protect the public weal.
They can not properly serve a mere group, least of all
themselves. We do not get our rights from them. Their
right to rule comes from us as the people.

The lesson of the past is plain in this connection. If
we neglect to exercise our legitimate control of those
whom we appoint to govern us, they will inevitably
exercise an unjust control of the whole people. They
will dictate to us even against our will. They will rule
as if they had a divine right to rule, and that is autocracy.

We must not, even in our greatest need, forget the nice controls, the careful checks and balancing of powers, so prudently and patiently worked out in our democracy. And if the need sometimes demands a large grant of power to our chosen rulers, we must watch the time when that need ceases and retrieve the temporary grant.

"All men are created equal: They are endowed by their Creator with certain inalienable rights, among which are life, liberty, and the pursuit of happiness." These are the constituent principles of our democratic heritage. They are not obvious truths; they are dogmas, but their truth underlies all our liberty and sound laws.

May God preserve to us our heritage of law and the liberties bound up with it. May He bless and protect the writers, interpreters, custodians and guardians of the laws by which our heritage and our liberties are secured. No less than spiritual authority, civil authority comes from God. It comes from God through the people, to be sure, but it remains divine and it entitles to our respectful obedience and fervent prayers all those elected to serve God and man with civil authority. To forget the divine origin of authority and the respect due its holders is to endanger democracy. To gather before the altar publicly to bear witness to these truths, as we do in the Red Mass, is to refresh and to strengthen the roots of democracy.

The
Common Good

CHAPTER V

ONE OF THE MOST BASIC QUESTIONS IN all social philosophy is this: Does society exist for each one of us, or does each one of us exist for society? Which, if either, of two goods provides the criterion of right or wrong, of morality and legality: the good which the *individual* needs and seeks for himself or the good which the *State* requires and seeks for itself?

Does the State, the organized society, exist for me; or do I, the individual citizen, exist for the State?

It is largely by their answers to these questions that many in our generation align themselves to the "Left" or to the "Right" on the social, economic, and political questions which agitate our thought. Moral and legal philosophies at the moment tend to polarize around one or the other of seemingly contrary and sometimes conflicting goods: the good of the *individual* and the good

[41]

of the *collectivity*. Those who are preoccupied with the primacy of individual good tend to take their stand or find themselves accounted with the parties of the "Right" in our era of State socialism. Those who opt for the *collective* good, and consequently give place of primacy to the rights of the State, turn up in our day in the ranks of the "Left."

Unfortunately the social philosophies to the "Left" and those to the "Right" have polarized at their extremes, with a consequent antagonism, bitter in its sharpness, between those in both camps who might normally be reasonable moderates. This antagonism is reflected in the spirit of suspicion with which men who disagree, however slightly, on social legislation, approach one another. It is reflected also in the intemperate name-calling by which men of conservative instinct or judgment increasingly find themselves dismissed as "Fascists" or "Reactionaries," while those of more liberal impulse or vision find themselves decried as if they were all "Revolutionaries" or "Anarchists."

Even more disastrous is the manner in which, as a consequence, extremists on every side become the symbols and spokesmen of the camps with which they are identified, even when they are neither typical nor worthy representatives of these camps, being more often than not unwelcome nuisances to their own side of "center."

Unfortunate, too, is the widespread sense of guilt, of "guilt by association," among sincere political "conservatives" and honest social "liberals" who find themselves isolated from equally honorable and sincere citizens in opposite political or social camps, isolated from good men to whom they are inhibited from stretching out the hand of collaboration because of the sharply polarized divisions of contemporary opinion. This paralyzing sense of guilt is intensified, to the great hurt of all concerned, by the embarrassment these same men find in the intellectual and moral company which they must keep on their *own* side of "center" as a result of this polarized condition of which they are themselves the victims. And so, high-minded so-called "liberals" are too often associated in popular opinion, if not always in fact, with actual or potential traitors; while great-hearted "conservatives" are frequently distressed to find themselves tarred with the same stick as bigots, misanthropes and the hard-of-heart generally.

Hence, it comes to pass, to the very great hurt, I repeat, of all concerned, that upright men find themselves unable to meet with one another on questions of either public or personal good, while they appear compelled to associate with evil companions almost fatally acquired in the pursuit of *good:* individual good in the case of the political "conservative," the collective good in the case of the social "liberal." Conscientious citizens find themselves discredited because they sought to liberalize where a broader, more generous mood in social legislation was clearly necessary, or to conserve where a more cautious or critical spirit was the manifest need of the hour.

What to do? How find a formula which can reconcile goods which are apparently in conflict, a formula under which we can rally to the service of America and of Christendom all the spiritual energies and intellectual resources which are now dissipated by polarized divisions disastrous alike to personal interest and to collective well-being?

The time-tested philosophy of Christendom, blending the hope of Hebrew prophecy, the wisdom of Greek speculation, the sanity of Roman law and the charity of Christian Revelation, had a phrase which provides the saving word. That philosophy spoke of a third good, a good wider than that of the individual and more warm than that of the collectivity; a good with richly personal elements, yet truly public in its nature. That third good, conciliating and unifying, is more humane than the mere good of the State; it is more generous than the good of the mere individual. It is, to repeat, both personal and public, though not merely individual on the one hand nor merely political on the other. It is what the scholastic philosophers of Christendom and the Founding Fathers of America called "the common good." Perhaps it is time to seek a reaffirmation of its nature and its claims.

We are not met for a class of philosophy, and so we may only suggest points for meditation elsewhere on the notion of the common good. You will find it in Aristotle, who strove to set a happy balance between the general good and private good, between the obligation of the individual to yield to the honest good of the political State and the obligation of the ·political State in turn to serve the individual good of what he called the "contemplative," i.e., the "spiritual" person.

You will find it in St. Thomas, who emphasizes the primacy of the common good in the practical or political order of the life of the community, but points out how the collective good and the State itself must ultimately subserve the nature and needs of the immortal person. Both the pagan Greek and the Christian philosopher understood that there is a sense in which the good of the whole is "more divine" than the good of the individual, but they also understood how the good of the social whole must be subordinated to the good of personality. They found the middle term for the equation between the individual good and collective good, between the spiritual good of the person and the political good of the State, in the term "the common good," a good which is not identified with any individual and yet which is not so identified with the collectivity, above all with the State, that it becomes detached from the true good of the person.

What is this "common good" devotion to which may yet rally in a single cooperative effort generous "conservatives" and thoughtful "liberals"? It is not, we have said, merely individual, though it is personal; it is not coldly political, though it is shared by all the body politic and includes many political elements. That which constitutes the common good of political society, Maritain

reminds us,* is not only the collection of public com-
modities and services — the roads, ports, schools, etc.,
which the organization of common life presupposes; it
is not merely a sound fiscal condition of the State and
its military power; the body of just laws, good customs
and wise institutions which provide the nation with its
structure; the heritage of its great historical remem-
brances, its symbols and its glories, its living traditions
and cultural treasures. The common good includes all
of these and something much more besides — something
more profound, more concrete and more human. For it
includes also, and above all, the whole sum itself of
these; a sum which is quite different from a simple collection of juxtaposed units. Even in the mathematical
order, as Aristotle points out, six is not the same as
three plus three. A victorious army is immeasurably more
than the mere physical total of the strength or even
the valor of the individuals who compose it. A symphony
orchestra is made up of so many players plus the con-
ductor, but the whole in this case is much more than
the mere sum of its parts.

So the common good includes the sum or sociological
integration of all the civic conscience, political virtues
and sense of right and liberty; of all the activity, material
prosperity, and spiritual riches; of unconsciously opera-
tive hereditary wisdom; of moral rectitude, justice, friendship, happiness, virtue, and heroism in the individual
lives of its members. For these things all are, in a certain

*The Person and the Common Good, Scribners, 1947, pp. 42 ff.

measure, communicable and so revert to each member, helping him to perfect his life and liberty as a person.

The common good so conceived is not only a collection of advantages and utilities, it is strongly moral and ethical in its content. It includes elements of rectitude and honor, of morality and justice. Only on condition that it embrace these is the common good truly such, namely: the good of a people living in a community, the good of an organized human city, rather than the mere booty shared by a pack of thieves or the common hoard of a mob of gangsters.

For this reason, perfidy, the scorn of treaties and of sworn oaths, political assassination and unjust war, even though they may be useful or advantageous and in this sense practically good, actually contribute to the destruction of the true common good, the *bonum honestum* of which the ancients spoke.

Let Maritain be here again our guide. The common good, he reminds us, is always ethically good. Included in it, as an essential element, is the maximum possible development, here and now, of the persons making up the united multitude to the end of forming a people organized not by force alone but by justice. Historical conditions and the still inferior development of human society make difficult the full achievement of the ends of social life. But the end to which it tends is to procure the common good of the multitude in such a way that the individual as a *person* gains the greatest possible measure, compatible with the good of the whole, of real independence from the servitudes of nature. The economic guarantees of labor and capital, political rights, the moral virtues, and the culture of the mind, all these contribute through the common good to the realization of this individual independence.

The common good includes, we have seen, the cultural, historical, and spiritual heritage which is shared by the group, as opposed to the heritage particular to any individuals within the group. It is difficult to analyze the elements of this heritage, impossible to do so in a sentence. But every now and again someone speaks out above the general din of dissident individual voices and utters ideals common to us all, words expressive of our heritage of "common good." When such a one so speaks, his individual characteristics fade out completely; his words sum up a good that all deeply cherish; only the utterance is his alone, that and perhaps the beauty of the particular words by which he gives expression to the common thought.

For example, Abraham Lincoln was a Republican; he lived in a specific period of American history; he presents strongly individualistic traits; he was a partisan of the Northern cause in the War between the States; it is difficult sometimes to appreciate that millions of sincere Americans profoundly disliked some of his ideas, deplored many of his policies, distrusted him personally. But when he spoke at Gettysburg, he spoke for us all; for all Americans, for our citizens in every epoch, every political party, every part of the country. There is no

American who does not sense that the very stuff of our
national common good — all its elements, its spiritual
fibre and its political pattern are woven into the things
that Lincoln said at Gettysburg.

Woodrow Wilson was a Democrat. He, too, lived in
a particular period of our national history and a specific
phase of our emergence into the international community.
He had marked individual traits, many of which his
friends found amiable, others of which his critics found
distasteful. Whole areas of his political philosophy were
unacceptable to millions of his fellow citizens and some
of his policies provoked the resentment of many. Yet in
his public pronouncements, he frequently transcended the
inevitable limitations of himself, his times, and his political context. There is no one in this land who does not
feel the tug of a common chord which runs through the
hearts of us all when he reads the magnanimous phrasing
of Wilson's declaration of war against the German government and not the German people; or the exalted
address to the Military Academy at West Point in which
Wilson summarized so many of the elements of our
"common good" and linked them, as the common good
must always be linked, to the benign purposes of God
and to the secrets of God's Providence. Do you remember
his words? —

    . . . America came into existence for a par-
ticular reason. When you look about upon these
beautiful hills and up this stately stream, and

then let your imagination run over the whole body of this great country from which you youngsters are drawn, far and wide, you remember that while it had aboriginal inhabitants, while there were people living here, there was no civilization which we displaced. It was as if in the Providence of God a continent had been kept unused and waiting for a peaceful people who loved liberty and the rights of men more than they loved anything else, to come and set up an unselfish commonwealth. It is a very extraordinary thing. You are so familiar with American . . . history that it does not seem strange to you, but it is a very strange history nonetheless. There is none like it in the whole annals of mankind — of men gathering out of every civilized nation in the world on an unused continent and building up a policy exactly to suit themselves, not under the domination of any ruling dynasty or of the ambitions of any royal family; doing what they pleased with their own life on a free space of land which God had made rich with every resource which was necessary for the civilization they meant to build upon it.

So the common good is all the heritage from the past and all the hope for the future which good men share under God. Common to many, it is therefore *public;* perfective of the individual, it remains somehow *personal.* It calls the individual out of himself to share things with the general community, but it puts the resources of the general community at the service of the things closest to the personality of the individual. That is what Cicero meant when he defined the common good, the *res publica,* in terms of a nation's altars and hearths, of the spiritual and domestic values which center about these and which serve personality; *in aris et focis est res publica.*

It was out of this concept of the common good that our forefathers derived their notion of the great object of the State's existence. Hence, their fine old phrase "the common weal," a phrase perpetuated in the name by which they designated their civil communities, not by the cold, collective name so dear to the totalitarian, "the State," nor with any name of special interest or partisan emphasis, as "the Duchy" or "the Realm," — but "the Commonwealth" as in "The Commonwealth of Massachusetts."

It is the concept of the common good which is behind warm words like "mutual" in the preambles of so many national and state constitutions, and in other phrases so frequent in the texts of our basic laws, as that of my own State which provides "that all shall be governed by certain laws for the common good."

It is the good which is preserved and promoted by the nurse who braves individual infection in order to serve the common good; by the scientist who forfeits individual convenience in order to increase that good; by the parent who foregoes individual advantage in order to rear future citizens to enhance that good; by the saint who renounces individual pleasure in order to sanctify the common good; by the soldier who disciplines individual preference in order to defend the common good; by the party or regime or even the State which abdicates particular claims or narrow prerogatives in order to conciliate those who share a common good.

It is the good which King St. Louis of France loved when he subordinated both the instincts of self and the claims of his State to a higher common good shared with others. Perhaps you remember the incident; one thinks of it with wistful admiration as one reads the daily news. His counselors unanimously rebuked St. Louis for excessive generosity in giving to the English King land which the French had regained from British conquest. King St. Louis did not concede the English claims and he could easily have vindicated his own by force, but still he freely yielded the land. He said: "My Lords, the land that I give him I give not because I am under obligation either to him or to his heirs, but so that there may be mutual love between my children and his. And it seems to me that I am making good use of what I give him, since it makes us join hands in common love who were before at odds."

It is the good which another Catholic saint meant when he lamented those frozen words "mine" and "thine" — *frigida ista verba meum et tuum* — and rejoiced in the warm word *nostra*: "the things that are ours."

The common good: it is the mutual bond of all who

love the good, the true, and the beautiful; who seek good things, not evil; who seek the private good of persons and the collective good of the State, but the good of both in and under and through the Supreme Good, which is God. It is the good which God gives us all in order to keep us together, as opposed to the good that He gives us each to keep to ourselves. It is the good before which, on due occasion, both individual and State are obliged to bow: the "common good."

Out of a reaffirmation of the reality and claims of the common good there would come many results greatly to be desired. A quickened appreciation of the common good would turn the tide against the reckless setting of class against class, the irresponsible incitement of group against group. It would coordinate anew the interests and the efforts of labor *plus* management, tradesmen *plus* intellectuals, statesmen *plus* generals, as against the present so frequent pitting of good men against other good men in the conflicts of labor *versus* management, intellectuals *versus* tradesmen, statesmen *versus* generals within the same nation and presumably seeking the same common good.

Such an appreciation of the common good which unites, as against — or, rather, as *above* — all particular or factional or partisan goods which divide, would make possible the "vital center" for which certain political philosophers are pleading; a vital center which can exist only when honorable moderates of right and left prefer working with each other in behalf of the common good to working with extremists of their own respective camps, extremists who seek only the particular good after which their side aspires. Thus, the present polarized condition of society would be eased and social conservatives, anxious to preserve the heritage of the past, would have a common ground on which to meet and work with social liberals anxious to enlarge the hope of the future. The common good includes, in the phrase of Scripture, *nova et vetera*: the old heritage and the new hopes.

Thus, the conscientious citizen who walks a little left of center, freed from the embarrassment of constant association with senseless revolutionaries, should be able to make common cause in the quest for the common good with the no less honorable citizen who steers his course a little right of center and who is too often condemned as the friend of soulless reaction.

A clearer concept of the reality and the rights of the common good may also suggest a formula for planning a better international order, an order which will conserve the values of the established nations, but be enriched by other, perhaps more basic and more humane supranational values, as little by little we come to appreciate how much of our heritage from the past and our hopes for the future are shared within other nations by millions who seek the true common good of mankind.

Finally, a new emphasis on the nature of the common good will re-orient the minds of men toward other goods, higher goods which transcend mere private advantage or even temporal common weal. The longer men meditate the nature and the notion of the common good, the more surely will they come to understand that there is no true good so secular, so of the earth and earthly, but what it comes from God and has been hallowed by His Christ so that, by its consecrated use, it can be a means to Heaven. There is no common good, no truly human heritage or valid hope of any people, which lies outside God's Providence and which is not bound up with His purposes. There is no valid good which is not somehow predestined, however natural it be in itself, to find its place in the supernatural order which God has revealed and through which all things created are finally brought back to Him.

Surely it is not too much to ask that Catholics, whatever their political preferences or occasional legitimate partisan commitments, should be among the first to understand and to seek the common good. If an enlightened civic sense does not make them responsive to the nature and claims of this wider good, the universal instinct of their more catholic religious insight should make them more sensitive to certain spiritual implications of the notion of the common good. For we may well hope that, reflecting on the nature of the common good and seeking always its more perfect accomplishment, minds and hearts will be lifted up afresh through the *bonum commune* to the *Summum Bonum,* the source of all good, God Himself, third and deciding partner in all enduring agreements, marital, industrial, or international.

The Reign of Law

CHAPTER VI

THE SUBJECT OF MY SERMON IS SUG-
gested by a phrase in the prayer that the president of
the St. Thomas More Society, Mr. Artuso, has this year
prepared in accordance with the custom of the Society.
It is an admirable prayer, appropriate both to the highest
spirit of the legal profession and to the most urgent
needs of the times. It asks the reign of law, as opposed
to force, in all human affairs, personal, communal and
international.

Such a reign of law would be a fulfillment in the
political and social order of that petition which all Christians make when they recite the Lord's Prayer: "Thy
kingdom come! Thy will be done, on earth as it is in
heaven!" This petition of the Lord's Prayer has to do
primarily with the order of grace and of the supernatural;
the law that it presupposes and for the accomplishment

of which it prays, is that transcendental, supreme and sovereign law of God in which lie the perfection and the peace of all that God has made, ourselves included.

But the sovereign law of God for the accomplishment of which we ask when we pray: "Thy kingdom come! Thy will be done, on earth as it is in heaven!" includes and is echoed in that law of nature which is present in and demanded by the essential constitution of all created things. The Will of God becomes known to us through revelation, but reason also tells us many things about God's Will. The perfect reign of law in human affairs is possible only in proportion as men explore the sources and the sanctions of law by every means that faith and reason provide.

Hence the wisdom that we, imitating the Founding Fathers of our Republic, promote the reign of law by conscientious, prayerful study of the laws of nature and of nature's God, with the spirit of reason that explores the laws of nature and the spirit of faith that meditates the will of nature's God. Hence the timeliness, for a generation that urgently needs and desperately seeks the reign of law, of a revival of insight into and acceptance of that so neglected concept of natural law which the Holy Catholic Church has never ceased to vindicate as being not less authentic and binding than the law of Revelation itself.

When governments crumble and states decay, positive law all over the world becomes chaotic. More and more

then, civilization depends for survival on the recognition
of the validity of the natural law.

The idea of natural law is a heritage of Christian and
classical thought. It does not go back merely to the
philosophy of the eighteenth century, which more or less
deformed it, but rather to Grotius, and before him to
Suarez and Francisco da Vitoria; it goes further back to
St. Thomas Aquinas; and yet further to St. Augustine,
the Church Fathers and St. Paul; it even goes back to
Cicero, to the Stoics, to the great moralists of antiquity
and the great poets, notably Sophocles. Antigone is the
eternal heroine of natural law, which the Ancients called
"the unwritten law," and this is perhaps the name most
accurately suggesting its nature.

Since a church is no place to discuss nonsense, we shall
take it for granted that most lawyers admit that there
is a human nature, and that human nature is essentially
the same in all men; it is difficult to see how lawyers
could seriously ply their trade in the absence of such a
basic conviction. One takes it for granted, too, that the
courts necessarily assume that man is gifted with intelligence and, therefore, acts with an understanding of what
he is doing and a power to determine for himself the
ends which he pursues.

On the other hand, constituted with a given, determi-
nate nature, man obviously possesses ends which correspond to his natural constitution and which are the same
for all—as musical instruments, whatever their particular
type and wherever they may be, have as their end the

production of certain attuned sounds. If they do not produce such sounds, they must be tuned or adjudged defective. But since man is endowed with intelligence and determines his own ends, it is within his powers to put himself in tune with the ends demanded by his nature. This means that there is by very virtue of human nature, an order or a disposition which human reason can discover and according to which the human will must act in order to attune itself to the necessary ends of the human being. The unwritten law, or natural law, involves, then, the disposition to discover and to correspond with such an order of nature.

Certain philosophers of pagan antiquity knew, Jewish and Christian thinkers know even better, that nature comes from God, and that therefore the unwritten law echoes the eternal law which is Creative Wisdom itself. That is why the idea of natural law or the unwritten law has linked in Western thought a sentiment of natural piety to that profound and sacred respect unforgettably expressed by Antigone.

Because they understand the real principle behind the natural law, acceptance of it should be more firm in those who believe in God than it may be in others, but even mere analysis of human nature and of the freedom of the human being should in itself demonstrate that there is an unwritten law behind all efforts to bring to pass the reign of law among men; that natural law is something as real in the moral realm as the laws of growth and senescence are in the physical order.

But law and knowledge of the law are two different things. The man who does not know the law (so long as this ignorance itself does not spring from culpability) is not responsible before the law. Moreover, knowing that there is law does not necessarily mean knowing what that law is. The natural law is written, we assert, in the heart of man, and this is broadly true. But this law is in the hidden depths of our hearts, as hidden from us as our secret hearts themselves. The metaphor of a law "written" in our hearts has itself been responsible for a great deal of obscurity, causing natural law to be represented as a ready-made code rolled up within the conscience of each one of us, which each one of us has only to unroll for himself and of which all men should naturally have an equal knowledge.

Natural law is not, in fact, a written law. Men know it with greater or less difficulty, and in different degrees, running the risk of error here as elsewhere. The only practical knowledge all men have naturally and infallibly in common is that we must do good and avoid evil. This is the preamble and the first principle of natural law; it is not the law itself. Natural law is the sum of things to do and not to do which follow from this first principle in necessary fashion, all because of the simple fact that man is man, nothing else being taken into account.

That every sort of error and deviation is possible in the determination of such moral obligations merely proves how fallible is unaided human reason and how easily sense and sensuality can corrupt our judgment.

Montaigne liked maliciously to remark that, among certain peoples, incest and thievery were considered virtuous acts. Pascal was scandalized by this. We are scandalized in our day by the fact that cruelty, denunciation of parents, the lie for the service of the political party, the murder of old or sick people, the aborting of human life should be considered virtuous actions by people acting under positive law inspired by atheistic scientism. All this proves nothing against natural law, any more than mistaken bookkeeping — or falsified bookkeeping — proves anything against arithmetic, or than the mistakes of primitive peoples, for whom the stars were holes in the tent which covered the world, prove anything against astronomy.

The natural law is an unwritten law. Man's knowledge of it increases little by little as man's moral conscience develops. After the Fall of Man, this moral conscience appears to have passed through a twilight state. As a result, the idea of natural law, for a time obscured in superstitious mythology, differentiated itself only slowly, as slowly as the idea of nature itself. The knowledge which our own moral conscience has of this law is doubtless itself still imperfect; it will no doubt continue to develop and to become more refined as long as humanity exists. Only when the Gospel has penetrated every level of human thought and being will natural law, properly understood, appear in its clarity and perfection.

Here is the great social contribution of the Teaching

Church. Here is why even the unbeliever should rejoice
that the Church functions, in these revolutionary times,
as the champion of the natural law as well as the defender
of the deposit of faith.

The devout understand that our full and final hope
for the coming of the reign of law lies in loving obedience to the Will of God made known to us in revelation
and accepted by devout faith; such loving faith is the
perfection of the law. But no small part of our hope
for the reign of law, its firm foundation on the level
of nature and reason, lies in the recognition of the
validity of that natural law to the existence and the
dictates of which reason is witness. The return to natural
law concepts carries with it our best hope, apart from
the revival of religious faith and the acceptance of Revelation itself, for the advent of the reign of law in the
international community. For unless something in the very
nature of man and of society dictates at least such basic
obligations as, for example, that the pledged word is
to be kept, that contracted obligations are in themselves
binding, (*pacta sunt servanda*) then, in fact, there is no
alternative to force and therefore to violence as the
ultimate sanction in human affairs; no peace save an
armed peace, always precarious and often disturbed, can
be possible unless the reign of law can have sanctions
on the level of reason — and this means unless the
natural law is valid.

In the validity of the natural law, as the mirror of
the Will of God for the things which He has made and

the pledge that we can discover that Will more perfectly through faith, lies, then, our best hope for the reign of law in the human community, international and national; in business; in the family and in personal affairs. Only if positive law corresponds to something in the very heart of men, in the very nature of his being, can it finally prevail; only when the laws that men write somehow match the law that God has implanted in creation itself will there be that harmony between human striving and divine purpose which we can properly call the reign of law and in which we can hope to find our peace.

Reasonable men, skilled in the law, who are also devout men, deeply in love with God, are the men upon whom the free world and all humanity must depend for the triumph of the reign of law over the conflicts of force and the chaos of violence.

The Philosophy
of
Responsibility

CHAPTER VII

"GOD MADE MAN FROM THE BEGINNING, and left him in the hand of his own counsel. . . . He shall have glory everlasting. He that could have transgressed, and hath not transgressed; and could do evil things, but hath not done them" (Ecclus. 15:14).

The trials of the so-called war criminals have been subjected to thoughtful criticism by commentators, legal philosophers, and historians. The opinion has been expressed that these "trials" may eventually cause our nation and our allies grave embarrassment because the courts which conducted them functioned without previous written law and with the doubtful competence of conquerors. Quite possibly, too, the cases of individual "war criminals" may have involved injustices or inequities because of passion, partisanship, or misrepresentation.

Whatever of all this, there was one refreshing aspect

to the determination to bring to trial the "war criminals" and to demand an accounting before some bar of justice from some of those who by deliberate plan and conscious choice brought about the appalling evil that was World War II. This determination constituted a dramatic affirmation before all the world and under the most solemn circumstances, of a seriously neglected truth — the truth that political, social, and other moral disasters do not merely happen. They are not the blind results of inexorable fate. Even the most complex of these calamities are not the work of irresponsible mechanical forces alone. Just as great movements forward in the social history of mankind may be accurately attributed to the honorable actions of upright men, so the moral disasters which overtake men and nations must be attributed to the unfortunate use by responsible men of that freedom in which God created mankind from the beginning.

In the rise and fall of societies as in the personal salvation or damnation of individual men, the old truth enunciated by Sacred Scripture remains valid. It is a law of social history as well as a condition of individual salvation: "He shall have glory everlasting. He that could have transgressed, and hath not transgressed; and could do evil things, but hath not done them." This is the clue to man's perfection: "Before man is life and death, good and evil, that which he shall choose shall be given him" (Ecclus. 15:18). "Behold I set forth in your sight this day a blessing and a curse: a blessing if you obey the commandments of the Lord your God . . . a curse, if you obey not" (Deut. 11:26-28). This is the key to a nation's progress, its use of the freedom in which God made man from the beginning: "Jerusalem, Jerusalem, thou who killest the prophets, and stonest those who are sent to thee. How often would I have gathered thy children together, as a hen gathers her young under her wings, but thou wouldst not" (Matt. 23:37).

The determination to bring to justice the so-called war criminals constitutes, I repeat, a dramatic reaffirmation of the reality of free will and of personal responsibility for the moral consequences of individual actions. I speak of a *reaffirmation* because the philosophy of responsibility had lost something of its appeal, certainly in social thinking and possibly in legal thinking, in the generation immediately preceding the war.

There has always been the temptation to shuffle off accountability for moral defect. Shakespeare described and refuted it: "This is the excellent foppery of the world, that when we are sick in fortune, often the surfeit of our own behavior, we make guilty of our disasters the sun, the moon, and the stars: as if we were villains by necessity; fools by heavenly compulsion; knaves, thieves, and treacherers, by spherical predominance; drunkards, liars, and adulterers, by an enforced obedience of planetary influence." *But* "the fault, dear Brutus, is not in our stars, but in ourselves, that we are underlings."

The philosophy of responsibility in modern times has further suffered from the impersonal, collectivist theories of society and of history which have found favor during and since the last century. These link human action more often to material forces and mass controls than to spiritual personality and individual responsibility. An earlier generation of devout and God-fearing people had recognized the challenge of some environments and the limitations of certain heredities, but they still acknowledged that the generality of men remained free to make conscious choice between moral life and death, between good and evil. But then social theory followed new lines along which it has attempted to lead legal theory and application. As against the old philosophy of responsibility there has grown up the theory that misconduct is always abnormal, that what the law calls crime and what conscience calls sin are to be explained largely in terms of causes beyond the control of the sinner or the criminal. The philosophy of responsibility has been replaced by the philosophy of excuse.

Under the newer concept, it is no longer a question of being able to transgress but refusing to do so; it is rather a question of acting in accordance with the characters which, without our asking, we have received. Character is considered a product of circumstances, and delinquency and crime are simply other names for conflict and maladjustment. Criminals are sick people, like the insane. They should be dealt with as sick people and, far from seeing in their criminal actions anything for which they are responsible, we must learn to recognize in criminality the existence of something for which society is responsible. This has become the typical doctrine of a whole school of "psychology" and "sociology."

Last month I listened to a broadcast over a national
network of an extremely effective radio drama. It was
clearly conceived by its author and presented by its broad-
casters as setting forth a profound and cogent point. Its
scene was the cell of a condemned murderer. Every
device of skillful radio-theater drove home the play's idea
as stated by one of the players: "Tonight I am sitting
on the edge of a prison cot in the cell of a condemned
murderer. Between him and the rope which will break
his neck and choke the breath from his throat are nine
hours of tortured darkness. Soon the collective hand of
society will reach out and pull the lever that will spring
the trap and send his feet kicking in mid-air in the death
struggle. Perhaps the collective conscience of society
will permit itself a slight qualm. As I write the murderer
watches me. He is nothing more than a big-boned, hulk-
ing, somewhat dull kid who continually trembles. He
will die in the first light of the morning. I shall write
then about the court which should have tried him. It is
a purely imaginary court, one which sits in judgment on
ordinary people who lead what might be called blameless
lives. This court was established by a law which reads
in part: 'Whereas the state decrees that no one lacking
twenty-one full years in age, can now alone be held
responsible for any murder, it is ordered that a minimum
of six shall then be hanged if one such minor is condemned to die.' And so this court has been called to find
quickly the necessary five: the five additional nooses

which await along with the one which society has decreed for this young murderer."

The five extra nooses, as the play developed, were fashioned for the necks of the boy's school principal, one of his parents, a political leader in his community, a representative of organized entertainment, and an average member of the general community. The broadcast was extremely effective. It undoubtedly left in the minds of millions the impression that thus responsibility was at last placed where it always belongs; not with the individual criminal, but with the total society — and therefore with no one. It was a dramatic example of the philosophy of excuse as opposed to the philosophy of responsibility.

Judge John Perkins, former Justice of the Boston Juvenile Court, tells how one morning a probation officer came into his court room and said: "I went to the prison association dinner last night. The principal speaker made a moving address. At the end of it, after describing how a parolee had committed an atrocious murder, he burst into a dramatic peroration. Raising his eyes to the ceiling and with his voice trembling with emotion, he exclaimed dramatically: 'Somehow, somewhere, someone of us failed this man.'" The judge remarked ironically: "You mustn't object to that argument. As a matter of fact, it is a wonderful idea for us, too. All these cases we have been worrying about, because they turned out badly, were not our fault. We never failed. Whenever we thought we had failed, some one else had always failed *us*."

This is the philosophy of excuse — the philosophy of ultimate irresponsibility. For more than a generation it has undermined the moral and legal and individual social responsibilities upon which the stability of society must repose.

The linking of misbehavior to maladjustments and to forces beyond the control of the individual offender may frequently be justified, but not so often as to warrant a general philosophy of law which loses sight of the normal facts of individual responsibility and of personal freedom. Misbehavior, whether sinful or criminal, always includes an element of maladjustment, but sometimes there are adjustments which the individual must make on the level of the spiritual in order to meet the test of the material and the trial of the evil.

We must ameliorate bad conditions. We must strive by social action to lighten the load where it is unjust or unsafe, but we must recognize that in all this adjustment there are adjustments expected of the individual as well. We have rationalized too many ruthless tyrants in terms of their adolescent frustrations. Too many maladjusted criminals have been explained in terms of the conflicts and tensions of potentially great artists who were forced to be obscure paperhangers in Austria or of potentially great leaders of social movements who became instead gangsters and leaders of anti-social rackets which tore American communities apart. Too much gangsterism and sheer criminality on the obscure levels of the underworld and on the higher levels of international war and diplomacy have been encouraged by this philosophy of excuse in the realm of conscience and in the courts. The war crimes trials have caused to resound in our century some echo, at least, of that voice of responsibility which spoke centuries ago with accents divine: "This night do they require thy soul of thee." They have reminded public servants of that accountability which is imposed on every free agent: "How is it that I hear this of thee? Give an account of thy stewardship, for now thou canst be steward no longer."

It is good for civilization that the philosophy of responsibility should be reaffirmed and that the philosophy of excuse should be subordinated to it, cut down to size. Civilization was not achieved by any such philosophy as that of excuse, by vagueness about accountability. Mankind did not emerge from recurring periods of social decline and even savagery by any such formulas. Social progress has not been accomplished by impersonal destinies, by the wave of the future, by the blind operation of uncontrolled, biological, economic, or social forces. It has been achieved by the vision and determination, by the self-knowledge and self-discipline of single individuals and of individuals in groups who have understood the meanings of these responsible, constructive words: *I know. I will. I do.*

" ' Lord, if thou wilt, thou canst make me clean.' And stretching forth His hands Jesus touched him saying: 'I will: be thou made clean.' And immediately his leprosy was cleansed" (Matt. 8:1-4). "And returning to himself, he said. '. . . I will arise, and will go to my Father, and say to Him: "Father, I have sinned against heaven and before Thee. I am not worthy to be called Thy son; make me one of Thy hired servants" ' " (Luke 15:17-19).

"It is for us, the living, rather to be dedicated here to the unfinished work which they who fought here have thus far so nobly advanced. It is rather for us to be here dedicated to the great task remaining before us — that from these honored dead we take increased devotion to that cause for which they gave the last full measure of devotion — that we here highly resolve that these dead shall not have died in vain — that this nation, under God, shall have a new birth of freedom — and that government of the people, by the people, for the people, shall not perish from the earth." (Lincoln, Gettysburg Address.)

"Poverty is the northwind that lashes men into Vikings. . . . What we call evils, as poverty, neglect, and suffering, are, if we are wise, opportunities for good. . . . If I am left alone, yet God and all the heroic dead are with me still. If a great city is my dwelling place, the superficial life of noise and haste shall teach me how blessed a thing it is to live within the company of true thought and high resolves. Whatever can help me to think and love, whatever can give me strength and patience, whatever can make me humble and serviceable, though it be a trifle light as air, is opportunity, whose whim it is to hide in unconsidered things, in chance acquaintances and casual speech, in the falling of an apple, in floating weeds, or the accidental explosion in a chemist's mortar." (John Lancaster Spalding, "Opportunity.")

It is easy to satirize these valiant concepts of an age perhaps more rhetorical, but also more resourceful, more self-reliant, more imbued with the philosophy of responsibility, more contemptuous of the philosophy of excuse. But the whole history of human achievement gives meaning to that rhetoric and attests to the worth of those who indulged it, who taught their children and told their fellow citizens and trained themselves to recognize that they could do evil, but must not; that they could transgress, but would not.

So we in our legislation, in our law courts, and in our social theory must recognize and make allowance for the inadequate and the unfortunate, but we must not treat their condition as the normal condition of mankind and we must not spin our moral philosophy around their deficiencies. In our sympathy we must not place emphasis on excuse rather than on responsibility and thus spread a demoralizing social philosophy. We must make responsibility the universal norm and excuse the challenged exception. We must state the rules rather than constantly find reasons why they do not apply. We might well return to a bit of the rhetoric that glorified heroism and achievement and tone down the rhetoric lavished on those who lack the moral wherewithal by which to try or who, having it, prefer to serve themselves and blame society rather than serve society and honor themselves. We must recognize how the philosophy of responsibility enabled boys with withered legs to become useful citizens, leaders of their community, but above all masters of themselves; while the philosophy of excuse has allowed men of real intelligence and potential parts to become the instruments of society's confusion and of their own damnation. Social stability and individual salvation still depend on the recognition of the central place of individual responsibility in whatever good may be accomplished or whatever evil must be suffered on the face of the earth over which God gave man dominion.

Specifically, it was the philosophy of responsibility that made America great. It is the basis of free self-government, as free self-government in turn has been the basis of American greatness. Woodrow Wilson said some wise things about the relationship of self-government to the kind of character produced by the philosophy of responsibility. He said: "Self-government is not a mere form of institution, to be had when desired, if only the proper pains are taken. It is a form of character. It follows on the long discipline which gives a people self-possession, self-mastery, the habit of order and peace and common counsel which will not fail them when they themselves become the makers of law."

I offer this as a legitimate social and political conclusion from the moral philosophy of responsibility: If we are to acquire or keep the kind of character which Wilson said was essential for self-government, we must preserve the disciplines by which that character is built and the moral philosophy which dictates those disciplines. Church, State, and home must unite in happy understanding to teach each generation the "self-possession, self-mastery, the habit of order and peace and common counsel which will not fail them when they themselves become the makers of law." Thus will our citizenry become the men of glory who could transgress, but will not do so; who could do evil things, but will not do them; who use their freedom, fortified by God's grace, to do God's will on earth unto the temporal stability of their nation and the eternal salvation of their souls.

Fear and Love
in the
Observance of Law

CHAPTER VIII

". . . GIVE PLACE TO THE FEAR OF THE Most High, for the fear of God is all wisdom" (Ecclus. 19:18).

"Much peace have they who love thy law, nor is it a stumbling block for them" (Psalm 118:165).

Ours is an age of fear. The fears of the age are the more pathetic because they are so largely wasted. Fear of the bomb, fear of the future, fear of death, fear of the other fellow, usually lead only to frenzy and to frustrated disorder, especially if they are the only kind of fear we know. Paranoid fear is wasted fear.

Fear could be healthy if once again it were holy; much personal and social constructive good could be accomplished by prudent, saving fear with healthy objects and holy roots. A revival of the old-fashioned, salutary and well-founded fear of the Lord might help

[76]

restore order to the lives of individuals who, in moral matters, now boast that they are "afraid of nothing." Such fear of the Lord would be a source of new and needed strength to our civilization, presently menaced by evils and the fear of evils which a people filled with the fear of the Lord, and of Him only, could meet with spiritual dignity and confident triumph. Finally, a revival of the fear of the Lord would help restore a fear of the sanctions of all law, local, national, and international, among a generation for whom the law is now held in cynical contempt, with consequent peril to our society from within almost as great as that which threatens it from without.

Sometimes it is said that motives of fear of the law and its sanctions are unworthy of free men and unproductive of true virtue. It is argued that only loyalty and observance inspired by love are worthy of the free person and productive of the good society. Even St. Gregory the Great can be quoted as having said: "We do not render true service to God so long as we believe from fear and not from love." And so it is argued that, in the civil society, we should tone down the sanctions which appeal to fear and rely on that education which produces love in order to bring about the observance of law and the achievement of order.

But so great a disjunction between fear and love is not well founded; we fear to lose that which we truly love — and we love that which we truly fear to lose, whether good name, freedom, our friends and families, life, or God Himself. Neither can we consider well-founded the implication that all fear is unhealthy in the good society and unworthy of the free man. There is a fear that is morbid and deranging, but there is also a fear that is healthy and constructive because it is inspired by the love of God as our supreme good and is motivated by the fear of losing Him. Such is that fear of the Lord of which the Sacred Scriptures speak so often and which is linked to the love of the law, the divine law and all positive law which follows from the human effort to apply the divine law.

Sacred Scripture speaks a psychologically sound as well as a revealed religious truth when it associates the fear of the Lord and the love of the law. "The fear of the Lord shall prolong (our) days . . ." (Prov. 10:27); "In the fear of the Lord is confidence of strength . . . (Prov. 14:26); "The fear of the Lord is a fountain of life . . ." (Prov. 14:27); "The fear of the Lord is wisdom and discipline . . ." (Ecclus. 1:34); "The fear of the Lord is the beginning of wisdom . . ." (Psalms 110:10); "But love is the fulfillment of the law (Rom. 13:10), [therefore] "let thy glory be in the fear of God" (Ecclus. 9:22).

And so, the fear of the Lord, efficacious and ennobling, is in fact bound up with love; it has its origin in the love of the good that is God, God whom we dread to lose. It is so intimately related to our love of God that we should speak not of fear *or* love, but of fear *and* love in the observance of the law and the achievement of order. Logically and psychologically there must be elements of both fear and love in the observance of the law so long as we are wanderers on the face of the earth. Only when we are confirmed in grace, secure in salvation so that nothing we cherish will be lost, can love be free of all trace of fear. That is why the Church teaches us to pray: "Grant O Lord, that we may have a perpetual fear and love of Thy Holy Name . . . " (Collect for the Second Sunday after Pentecost), in order that our spiritual, supernatural salvation may be achieved.

Such, by analogy, should the good citizen's attitude be toward the majesty of the law and the accomplishment of a decent order in the good human society. His attitude should be a blend of wholesome fear and a certain holy love, motivated by a recognition that, on every level, fear is the beginning of wisdom and love is its perfection. "The fear of God is the beginning of his love" (Ecclus. 25:16) ; "the care of discipline is love, and love is the keeping of her laws and the keeping of her laws is the firm foundation of incorruption" (Wis. 6:19)

So do healthy fear and holy love, both of God and of His world, blend to produce a wholesome attitude toward the law. So also should they blend to produce a positive, confident reaction to the problems of our times. The widespread morbid fears of the moment are paralyzing to the forces of faith and freedom; it was doubtless intended that they should have precisely this effect, for they are fears aroused and exploited by the rocket-rattlers and the bomb-jugglers who alone can gain from the hysteria around us. This hysteria in itself reveals the presence in our civilization of the kind of fear against which Christ warned in words that He might well have chosen precisely for our generation. Christ said: "I say this to you who are my friends: Do not be afraid of those who can kill the body, and after that they can do no more. I will tell you who it is you must fear: fear Him who has power not only to kill but to cast a man into hell; Him you must fear indeed!" (Luke. 12:4-5).

Since these words of Christ retain their ancient truth, there is obviously a double need for the revival of the fear of the Lord in our day. It is needed to provide sanctions for a restored love of all law, human and divine, civil and sacred; but it is also needed in order to provide a healthy and holy perspective within which to view the threats of the hour and to control the morbid fears which rise from these.

This latter need is suggested by an interview with the Chief Secretary of the Communist Party and Prime Minister of Soviet Russia published by Mr. C. L. Sulzberger in the *New York Times.* Mr. Sulzberger posed to Mr. Khrushchev this searching question: "Don't you think that Communists, who are atheist by conviction and do not believe in Divinity or after-life, should therefore fear war more than religious people who do believe in some form of existence after death?" Khrushchev declared that he found the question a very interesting one; obviously it intrigued him. But it also irritated him and embarrassed him. He finally decided to dismiss it with superficial and cynical wisecracking about the failure of Gagarin and Titov to find angels or the Garden of Eden in the space through which they passed a little over one hundred miles above Moscow, Memphis, and Madrid. He remarked, moreover, that he had never noticed any special desire among religious people to get to heaven in a hurry!

This glib thrust at contemporary Western civilization should embarrass us to the extent that we have grown weak in the religious faith and therefore the spiritual power of our believing fathers, above all our heroic martyrs. The conquering faith they had in the future life explains the confident contempt that they had for the despots of this world; their religious, moral fear of God enabled them to live and to die without political fear of any man or physical fear of any material thing.

An essential point in the exchange between Sulzberger and Khrushchev may easily be missed in the midst of the flippancies of the Soviet dictator. The basic question of Sulzberger, which obviously would be a greater embarrassment to Khrushchev if our Western faith and morals were what they should be, turns on this: Which civilization is in the more advantageous position, spiritually and therefore politically: the civilization that has mastered the secrets of this world and yet fears the judgment of God in the world to come, or the civilization that has only mastered the secrets of this world and must fear to lose them and thus lose everything, since it denies the existence of God, despises His judgment, and has no hope beyond the world which it can annihilate but with which, by its own theory, it must forever perish?

In this case, the people with *two fears,* the believing people, are stronger even in temporal terms than the people, the non-believing people, who have only *one fear,* but that a fear necessarily involving ultimate despair. And so, if we of the West truly lived by our faith in the world to come and walked in fear of the judgment of God upon how valiantly we meet the evils of this world, we would be the more disposed and prepared to prevail over those who fear neither God nor man. But Khrushchev, though obviously troubled by what would be the advantage of a people truly inspired by faith and by fear of God, was unfortunately able to quip cynically that we probably have faith no more profound than his and that we therefore have fears no more efficacious or salutary than those of his atheists.

If this be true, then it is fatal to the future of our freedom as well as to the future of our faith. But if it is false, as I believe it to be—if we do truly fear God and love His holy law—then we have less reason to fear men or events and Mr. Khrushchev has more reason to invoke in private, as he so frequently does in public, the God in whom he professes not to believe.

Those who do not fear God, or love His law, or acknowledge Him, are not, on that account, without fear; quite the contrary, they live surrounded by fears, bedevilled by fears of everything but God, frenzied fears of the wrath of the living and the rivalry of the dead.

Fear and love join, then, with faith in the developing of sound attitudes toward all law and order. Moreover, the part of fear should not be underestimated, least of all despised. The holy fear of which we speak is perfectly consistent with and conducive to a sincere and efficacious love of the law. Fear of disgrace, fear of discovery in guilt, fear of offending those whom we love, all give important reinforcement to our human efforts to grow in virtue and in the love of the law. Fear of the Lord is the beginning of wisdom, even though love is its final perfection.

These truths concerning constructive fear are illustrated not only in the analysis of valid attitudes toward the law, but also in the effort to develop healthy attitudes towards our times. Here, too, fear can be morbid but it can also be healthy. In one of our cities a prominent medical man recently spoke of the pathetic fears which are prompting people to a tragic waste of time, money, and effort on what he described as absolutely worthless bomb-shelters. But he found even more pathetic the "unhealthy sense of security" that the very erection of these shelters brings with them.

So, too, there can be an unhealthy "sense of security" in moral matters, as when those who live in violation of the law or in contempt of its majesty, who are without fear of the Lord, feel falsely secure in the mistaken sense of well-being that comes from a comfortable, convenient but false assumption that God does not exist, or that His law is not relevant, or that, in any case, if He exists "He's a good fellow and 'twill all be well." Such a "sense of security" is not fearless; it is simply foolish. It can lead only to frightful disaster, moral and social.

To sum up: a holy and wholesome fear of the Lord would cut down to size other fears— military, political and personal—that so dismay and disorganize our society. It would restore some of the spiritual and moral valor that once made generations of men, filled with fear of the Lord, stand up boldly to outrageous fortune and to outrageous people, as Pius VII did to Napoleon and as our American forefathers did to the tensions and trials of days quite as bad as these. The fear of the Lord, deeply felt, devoutly followed, would promote our temporal security here below as well as secure our own eternal salvation hereafter. It would restore to human courts and to human law a majesty and respect that they inevitably lose when the fear of the Lord is forgotten.

Men who fear God have few other fears; men who love God's law hold all law sacred. There is a lesson for the times in the texts which we have meditated: ". . . Give place to the fear of the Most high, for the fear of God is all wisdom" (Ecclus. 19:19). "Much peace have they that love thy law, nor is it a stumbling block for them" (Psalm 118:165).

St. Thomas More and the Modern Lawyer

CHAPTER IX

"LET US NOW PRAISE MEN OF RENOWN, and our fathers in their generation . . . rich men in virtue . . . living at peace in their houses . . . Let the people shew forth their wisdom, and the Church declare their praise" (Ecclus. 44, passim).

The solemn, prayerful action of praise and petition which is the Red Mass brings before the altar of God the representatives of the bench and the bar, the members of the judiciary and of the legal profession. It unites them on the mystic level of prayer with those who, across the ages, have called down the blessing of the Supreme Lawgiver of the universe on the evolution of law in the universities and halls of justice of these twenty Christian centuries, for in all these has the Red Mass brought together the men who have fashioned our legal traditions.

It is appropriate that this Mass be offered today, for it

was on this day, twenty-two years ago, that thousands of us then present in St. Peter's witnessed the canonization in Rome of the saint who, in unparalleled manner, exemplifies the qualities and perfects the pattern we trust will characterize the men of the law who meet to pray with us this morning.

That saint is Thomas More. We do well to honor the coincidence between the anniversary of his canonization and this first Red Mass sponsored by Worcester county lawyers banded together in his name. We also do well to profit from the occasion by meditating briefly on the luminous lessons of More's earthly life and death, as well as his abiding life in the Church Triumphant. In the eternal life which is now his, Thomas More is an inspiration to all his brethren in the Church Militant and to all other men whose own clear minds and clean hearts impel them to show forth by imitation the wisdom of the saints and to praise, above all by the honest pattern of their own private and professional lives, the men of renown who are God's saints.

Who are the saints and what is their function in our lives? A modern writer puts it somewhat like this: From the beginning God intended us to walk before His face in holiness. But we could hardly know what holiness is, for our fathers became entangled in evil and error, and the fantasies of sin obscured the vision of sanctity within us and among us. And so, God sent His Son to live among us that whoever saw Him might see the holiness of the Father also. But as the years go by, even His likeness is continually darkened by human interpretations, painted over and distorted, until His features are scarcely discernible; we come to remember Him only on the level of doctrine, not as first we saw Him in the flesh and in the glory of His holiness. Then the saint comes, and lives the very life of Christ, as it were, before the eyes of those who share his circumstances, his work, and his manner and condition of life. He represents that life of Christ, so that each of us, seeing both something of Christ and something of himself in the saint, may glean and guess with longing how Christ would have lived had He been we and shared our walk in life.

This is the great function of the saints; this is the temporal point of our preaching the memory of their sublime merits. This is the greatest gift of the saints to us; not the stream of good deeds which they shower on the earth; or the great works of their hands, or the books of their wisdom, but that, because of them, the living likeness of the Master of Men, the hero of our race, the image of the glory of the Only Begotten of the Father, full of grace and truth, never quite disappears from the earth. Our saints, each in the context and calling he shares with us, reflects, to each of us according to our nature and need, that which God wills and our own best selves desire us to be.

Hence the great fascination and mighty example of a saint like Paul for the preacher of the word; of a saint like Francis for the servant of the poor; of a saint like King Louis for the wearer of a royal crown; of a saint

like Thomas à Becket for a churchman in times of bitter
conflict with the spirit of the world. Hence, too, the appeal of Thomas More to a layman who belongs to a
learned profession or is bound by public office and personal conscience to apply, to interpret, to plead, to practice, and himself to keep the law.

Who is this saint, this mighty man of God, who is the
exemplar and patron of your calling, this man the re-
production of whose merits and grace in any few of us
would be an abundant answer to the prayers of this Red
Mass? He was born in London in February, 1478; he
died there on July 6, 1535, executed by King Henry,
whom he had served with great intelligence and fidelity.
The son of a father himself enamored of the law, young
More became first the page and then the protégé of Arch-
bishop Morton, who loved him dearly and directed him
to Canterbury Hall, now Christ Church, at Oxford.

He studied the law in Lincoln's Inn, distinguishing
himself for his skill as a pleader and for the sharpness
and grace of his mind. Cardinal Wolsey, the arrogant
genius who succeeded in assuming to himself the symbols
of the power of both Pope and King, drew young More
into his civil service. The young man was shortly knighted
and taken into the privy council of the King. Successively
Treasurer of the Exchequer, Speaker of the House of
Commons, envoy to France, Chancellor of the Duchy of
Lancaster, he finally replaced the worldly Cardinal as
Lord High Chancellor, a post to which he brought scru-
pulous integrity and uncompromising loyalty. He resigned

the Great Seal when he could not in conscience acquiesce to Henry's divorce from Catherine of Aragon. Then, when finally the King was declared supreme head of the Church in England, More declined to take the oath of supremacy and paid with his head for his resistance to a totalitarian political pattern which has become so familiar in our later days. Sir Thomas accepted disgrace and death with cheer and with light-hearted banter that made outwardly merry his inward indomitable and austere adherence to the due order of values and to the proper primacy of principle, personal conscience, and the things of the spirit.

The King, moved by his many and great debts to Sir Thomas, as well as by affection for the man and the friend, softened the sentence for treason from hanging, disembowelling and quartering, to mere beheading, an act of grace which More received in his usual vein of ready wit. He ventured the good-humored hope that none of his friends might ever have occasion to experience like mercy from the King.

A scholar of varied and genuine erudition; an orator of ready and amiable eloquence; a friend of discriminating, warm affection; a lawyer and public servant of painstaking, assiduous, and learned skill; a spouse and father of exemplary virtue and provident, greathearted family spirit; one of the brightest personalities of the Renaissance, the Church offers him as an inspiration to you who officially preserve and promote the good order of this world, but who must not personally lose the good things of the world to come.

Such, in summary so brief that by it one only hopes to awaken your desire to read and reflect further on the full story of this man of renown, your forefather in the liberal and sound traditions of your craft, was the life of Thomas More.

Dean Swift said of him that he was "the person of the greatest virtue this Kingdom [of England] has ever produced." The Anglican scholar and clergyman, Dr. Hutton, declared it difficult to speak of More without using language which seems extravagant. Dr. Hutton found his character so beautiful, his life so simple and so pure, his conscientiousness so complete, his end so heroic, as to cause him to stand out among the sordid meannesses of the sixteenth century like a single star in the darkness of a world of disappointing popes, disagreeable kings, greedy statesmen, and spineless clergy.

Historical research, which has reversed to their disadvantage the judgment of the sixteenth century concerning so many of More's contemporaries, has but increased the moral stature of this layman in the Church and lawyer in the world, the luster of whose virtues and talents has grown with the passing centuries.

To present his moral portrait I might choose from widely diversified and otherwise almost mutually irreconcilable sources. I might, of course, cite the tribute in which the Pope of Rome lauded his memory in the moment of his canonization. But so, too, I might read you a letter from Moscow in which an institution bearing the name of Karl Marx communicates in our day with a convent of English nuns, seeking information on a mutual interest: the life and work of this so universally attractive scholar, social visionary, and intrepid saint. I might quote to you from the Socialist Karl Kautsky, or the Catholic Theodore Maynard; from Hollywood producer, John Farrow, or the Harvard Law School professor, Dean Roscoe Pound. But none would notably enhance nor, assuredly, reduce the estimate of More which Erasmus wrote while More was still alive.

It is not often that a priest finds sermons in the acid pages of Erasmus, yet one could not do better in sketching the ideal portrait of the devout member of a learned profession than to recall some pertinent passages from a letter that Erasmus wrote on Sir Thomas More:

> His house seems to have a sort of fatal felicity, no one having lived in it without being advanced to higher fortune, no inmate having ever had a stain upon his character.
>
> It would be difficult to find anyone living on such terms with a mother as he does with his stepmother. . . . His affection for his parents, children and sisters is such, that he neither wearies them with his love, nor ever fails in any kind attention.
>
> His character is entirely free from any touch of avarice. He has set aside out of his property what he thinks sufficient for his children, and

spends the rest in a liberal fashion. When he
was still dependent on his profession, he gave
every client true and friendly counsel, with an
eye to their advantage rather than his own, generally advising them, that the cheapest thing
they could do was to come to terms with their
opponents. If he could not persuade them to do
this, he pointed out how they might go to law
at least expense; for there are some people
whose character leads them to delight in litigation. . . .

It has always been part of his character to be
most obliging to everybody, and marvelously
ready with his sympathy; and this disposition is
more conspicuous than ever, now that his power
of doing good is greater. Some he relieves with
money, some he protects by his authority, some
he promotes by his recommendation, while those
whom he cannot otherwise assist are benefited
by his advice. No one is sent away in distress,
and you might call him the general patron of
all poor people. He counts it a great gain to
himself, if he has relieved some oppressed person, made the path clear for one that was in
difficulties, or brought back into favour one
that was in disgrace. No man more readily
confers a benefit, no man expects less in return.
And successful as he is in so many ways— while
success is generally accompanied by self-conceit,
I have never seen any mortal being more free
from this failing. . . .

It would be difficult to find anyone more successful in speaking *ex tempore,* the happiest thoughts being attended by the happiest language; while a mind that catches and anticipates all that passes, and a ready memory, having everything as it were in stock, promptly supply whatever the time, or the occasion, demands. In disputations nothing can be imagined more acute, so that the most eminent theologians often find their match, when he meets them on their own ground. Hence John Colet, a man of keen and exact judgment, is wont to say in familiar conversation, that England has only one genius, whereas that island abounds in distinguished intellects.

However averse he may be from all superstition, he is a steady adherent of true piety; having regular hours for his prayers, which are not uttered by rote, but from the heart. He talks with his friends about a future life in such a way as to make you feel that he believes what he says, and does not speak without the best hope. Such is More, even at Court; and there are still people who think that Christians are only to be found in monasteries!

What lessons shall we draw, pertinent for those present at a Red Mass and for our day, from the story of this so modern and so holy man? The lessons of More's life are many and for us all; they are, of course, particularly in point for members of the legal profession.

Of general interest is the striking parallel between certain aspects of his times and ours, between his destiny and what may easily be that, however secret and unsung, of many men in our day, even of some to whom I speak.

A popular biographer of More points the parallel between his time and our own, both ages of transition. In More's day the medieval order was yielding to the intellectual, political, and economic revolution of a new age, and Christendom was rent by the divisions between Protestant and Catholic. In our day Western civilization is on trial in the intellectual, political, economic, and spiritual spheres in resistance to the pressure of totalitarianism in every form. Thus it is easy to restate the central problem of More's destiny—that of liberty of conscience—in modern terms. The story of his life in a confused and changing society and his death on the scaffold, after a mock trial comparable to the course of Soviet justice, is of deep significance to every modern man.

But to members of the legal profession, the memory of St. Thomas More has special lessons for guidance, instruction, and consolation. One aspect of his record of achievement is of passing, perhaps whimsical interest, in view of the great mass of litigation before our courts today.

When More came to the Chancellor's Court he found a backlog of cases that had dragged on for twenty years. He vowed to remedy the situation and his vow was not lightly made. Eventually there came one welcome morning when he was informed by the officers of the court that there was no more unfinished business, not another cause or petition to be put before him. So was born a popular rhyme:

> When MORE some time had Chancellor been,
> No MORE suits did remain;
> The same shall never MORE be seen
> Till MORE be there again.

Clearly not the least of St. Thomas More's good examples to us is that which he gave against "the insolence of office and the law's delay"!

But more permanently significant and edifying to members of the profession in our day are certain other points for meditation which we may glean from the life of this lawyer-saint.

The first follows from the fact that the lawyer is a member of a learned profession. He is therefore called to a love for the things of the mind, and he is bound to play his part in keeping alive the authentic humanistic spirit exemplified in men like Thomas More. He must have a knowledge and love for the liberal arts, those traditional "humanities" which, with the grace of God, must save us from cold materialism and dehumanizing technocracy.

Only thus will the lawyer play his proper part in the cultural revolutions of our times, a part which should parallel that which More and his like played in the comparable upheavals of his age. A man of More's learning was inevitably attached to the values of the old order; his intellectual curiosity made him sensitive to those of

the new. He had no part with those who would defend
the old Faith only with outmoded weapons inconsistent
with and inadequate to the demands of the new learning
and the new methods. But neither would he cast his lot
with those who, swept off their feet by the new ideas
and new methods, became insensible, indifferent, and
finally renegade to the imperishable values of the old
Faith.

A devoutly humanist spirit like that of More, bold yet
humble, venturesome in vision yet steadfast in attachment to old truths, is a primary need of the learned pro-
fessions in our own changing times.

Second, the professional man, the man in public life,
remains a family man. His obligations to his career and
his commitments to his public office do not exempt him
from his primary duty to be the head of his family, the
companion of his spouse, the first and best educator of
his own children. In this, the example of your patron is
luminous and timely.

By the time he had reached his thirty-fifth birthday,
Thomas More had achieved a state of living that would
have satisfied the aims of most men. He was a lawyer
with a wide and lucrative practice. As Under-Sheriff he
had gained an envied position in the city of London. He
was a popular "bencher" among his colleagues at Lincoln's Inn. He was an acknowledged scholar with a large
circle of distinguished friends. But he took pains to be
a fond parent and a considerate husband.

In a letter to a friend he wrote: "For while in pleading,

in hearing, in deciding causes, or composing disputes as an arbitrator, in waiting on some men about business, and on others out of respect, the greatest part of the day is spent on other men's affairs, the remainder of it must be given to my family at home . . . I must gossip with my wife and chat with my children, and find something to say to my servants; for all these things I reckon a part of my business, unless I were to become a stranger in my house. . . ."

One suggests, without offense, I hope, that many families of professional men in our day would be the more stable and proud if their fathers could give more of their time to their sons and daughters, more of their intimate, personal love and interest than of their mere money and indulgence.

Third, the citizen of this world, the servant of its powers and principalities, its kings or its democratic majorities, remains the subject and the servant of God. Of nothing, of course, was Thomas More more conscious; it is the pattern of his life and the point of his death. He could have been, as Wolsey was, the most powerful man in England, next only to the king, if he would have strained his conscience a bit on a point which, God help us, seems almost minor to our day and on which in his day churchmen compromised themselves.

In this, the contrast between the enlightened, sensitive nobility of the lawyer, Thomas More, and the sad deterioration of the prelate, Thomas Wolsey, is worth constant meditation by us all.

Wolsey and More were as unlike in many ways as men can be; in others they were curiously similar. Both were remarkable scholars, standing well out from their fellows. One, Wolsey, in scarlet magnificence, was to live with a splendor never seen before or since in England. The other, More, in hair shirt, singing in a parish choir, was to be criticized because of the modesty of his ways. One was to succeed the other as Lord Chancellor of England. Both were to win the fickle friendship of Henry VIII and both were to attract the petulant anger of young Anne Boleyn. "I die the King's good servant, but God's first," said More as he faced martyrdom, gracefully meeting death with a prayer, a quip, and a holy joy. "If I had served God as diligently as I have done the King," wept Wolsey at the end, "He would not have given me over in my gray hairs."

Here, surely is a lesson for our times, a lesson for me, for each of you, for all men, high and low, who ride this planet with us across the troubled universe of the twentieth century. What a glory for lawyers that one of their number should so instruct us! What a tragedy for us all, for the Church and for the State, if the pattern of such a life should be lost to us, whatever be our gains in these changing times!

Let us, then, praise this man of renown, our father in the profession; a man rich in virtue . . . living at peace in his house. . . . Let the lawyers show forth his wisdom, and the Church declare his praise!